DICK HAMILTON'S CADET DAYS

OR

THE HANDICAP OF A MILLIONAIRE'S SON

HOWARD R. GARIS

[ZHINGOORA BOOKS]

This edition is published by
Zhingoora Books.

PREFACE.

My Dear Boys:

When I had finished the first volume of this series, telling of the doings of Dick Hamilton, the young millionaire, I was in some doubt as to just how you would like it. I hoped that you would be pleased with it, and interested in Dick and his chums, and what they did, but I could not be sure of it.

That you did care for it, I am now assured, and I am glad to be able to give you the second volume, relating some of Dick's experiences while at a leading military school.

You will recall that, after he had come into possession of his great fortune, by fulfilling certain conditions of his mother's will, there were still other things for him to do; matters that his mother had planned before her death. One of these was to make sure that her son would get a good military training.

Dick went to Kentfield Academy, but, to his surprise, he met with a very cold reception from the other cadets. Ray Dutton, not understanding that, in spite of our hero's wealth, he was a fine chap, influenced the other students against Dick, and, for a time, the young millionaire was very lonely in the big school. But he resolved to fight his own battles, and become popular in spite of his wealth.

Uncle Ezra brought him bad news, but it was the means of great good luck for Dick, though Grit, the bulldog, seemed to regard the crabbed old man as his master's enemy, and chased him from the school.

All this you will find set down in the present volume, and also an account of how Dick was instrumental in locating a long missing soldier, and how, when the society house of the Sacred Pig burned down, without any insurance being in force, Dick, with his wealth, came to the aid of the surprised cadets.

Yours sincerely,

Howard R. Garis.

CONTENTS

CHAPTER

CHAPTER I

DICK GETS A TELEGRAM

"Hi boys! Here goes for a double summersault!"

"Bet you don't do it, Frank."

"You watch."

"Every time you try it you come down on your back," added another lad of the group of those who were watching one of their companions poised on the end of a spring-board.

"Well, this time I'm going to do it just like that circus chap did," and Frank Bender, who had an ambition to become an acrobat, raised his hands above his head and crouched for a spring.

"If you do it I'll follow," said another boy, clad in a bright red bathing suit.

"Good for you, Dick!" exclaimed Walter Mead. "Don't let Frank stump you."

"Here I go!" cried Frank, and, a moment later, he sprang from the spring-board, leaped high into the air, and, turning over twice, came down in true diver style, his hands cleaving the water beneath which he disappeared.

"Good!" cried the boys on the shore.

"I didn't think he'd do it," remarked "Bricktop" Norton, so called from his shock of red hair.

"Me either," added Fred Murdock. "Now it's up to you, Dick."

"That's right."

Dick Hamilton rose from a log on which he was sitting. He was a tall, clean-cut chap, straight as an arrow, with an easy grace about him, and it needed but a glance to show that he was of athletic build. His red bathing suit, from which protruded bronzed arms and legs, was particularly becoming to him.

"There—let's—see—you—do—that!" spluttered Frank, as he came up, some distance from where he had gone down. He shook his head to rid his eyes and ears of water, and struck out for shore.

"Stay there!" called Dick. "I'll swim out farther than you did."

"Dick's cutting out some work for himself," remarked Bricktop, in a low tone to Bill Johnson. "Frank's a dandy swimmer."

"Yes, but Dick Hamilton usually does what he sets out to do," replied Bill. "There he goes."

Dick walked to the end of the spring-board. He teetered up and down on it two or three times, testing the balance of the long plank. Then he took a few steps backward, poised for an instant, and ran forward.

"There he goes!" called Walter.

Like a rubber ball Dick Hamilton arose in the air. He curled himself up into a lump as he leaped, and then, to the surprise of his companions, he turned over not twice, but three times ere he struck the water, which closed up over his feet as they disappeared.

"Well—wouldn't that sizzle your side combs!" cried Bricktop. "Three times!"

"A triple!" added Walter Mead. "Whoever would think Dick could do it!"

"Aw, he's been practicing," called Frank, as he circled about in the water, watching for Dick to come up. "He's been doing it on the sly, and he's kept quiet about it."

"Just like Dick," added Bill. "He isn't satisfied to do ordinary stunts."

"Well, he's done a good one this time," said Fred Murdock. "Say, isn't he staying under a long time?"

There was no sight of the millionaire youth.

"Maybe he hit his head on a rock," suggested Bricktop, in some alarm.

"That's so," went on Fred. "This place isn't any too deep, and he came down hard."

"Maybe we'd better go in after him," remarked Walter.

"Dive down!" called Bill to Frank.

The boys were becoming frightened. Not a ripple, save the little waves made by Frank, as he stood upright, treading water, disturbed the expanse of the swimming hole. There was no signof Dick Hamilton. Frank prepared for a dive, when, suddenly, at some distance from shore something shot up through the water. It was the hand and arm of a boy. An instant later his head and shoulders popped into view.

"There he is!" cried Walter.

"It's about time he came up," said Bill, somewhat sharply, for Dick's long under-water swim had frightened the boys.

"How's that, fellows?" asked Dick, as he shook the water from his face, and struck out for shore.

"You win!" cried Frank, "but please don't give us heart disease again."

"Why; what's the matter?"

"We'd thought you'd struck on a stone and weren't going to come up again."

"No danger of that," answered Dick, with a laugh. "I'm having too much fun at camp here, to stay down there. Did I make a good dive?"

"Did you? Say, you've got us all beat to a pig's whisper on Fourth of July," admitted Bricktop. "How'd you do it?"

"Yes, I wish you'd show me," added Frank. "You must have been practicing it."

"I have," admitted Dick. "It's easy when you know how. After you do a double summersault, all you have to do—is to make another one, making three in all, and you can see that I had nothing concealed up my sleeve, and——"

"And you did it without the aid of a net," added Fred, after the fashion of the ringmaster in a circus announcing some marvelous feat.

"I'm going to try it," said Frank, as he clambered out on the bank.

"No, I think we've been in the water long enough this morning," said Dick. "Besides it's most grub time. I don't know how you feel about it, but I think I could nibble at a bit of roast chicken, which I happen to know that our esteemed cook, Hannibal Cæsar Erastus Jones, has in the oven."

"Ah! Um!" murmured Bill Johnson.

"That's it! Make a noise like a lunch-grabber!" objected Fred. "I should think you'd be ashamed of yourself."

"Oh, listen to the professor at the breakfast table!" cried Bill with a laugh. "I don't s'pose you're going to nibble at any; art thou, Reginald?"

"Well, you just watch him," advised Fred. "He's got me beat, all right."

"Come on!" cried Dick suddenly. "First fellow at the dining tent gets most of the white meat!"

He started off at a fast clip, the others sprinting after him, and he would have won, but that he stubbed his bare toe on a stone, and had to finish the rest of the distance on one leg, holding the injured member in his hands, making, the while, wry faces at the pain. Bill Johnson won the impromptu race.

"Hurt much?" asked Walter, as Dick limped up.

"Like sin. Say, Hannibal Cæsar Erastus Jones, will you do me a favor?" he asked, as the colored cook, who did the camp cooking, came from his tent.

"Ob co'se, Massa Dick. What am it?"

"Just go back there in the woods and bring me the pieces of that stone I broke with my toe. I want 'em for souveniers."

"Ha! Ha! Ho! Ho! Massa Dick, doan yo' go to playin' no tricks on me! Not jest at de present auspicious moment," and the colored man grinned broadly, showing a big expanse of white teeth, in an area of blackness.

"Why not, Rastus?"

"'Case as how de chicken am all done, an' if it ain't partook of immejeet——"

"Never mind those souveniers," said Dick. "We'll be with you in the twinkling of a flea's left hand eyelash," and he hopped into his tent, and began to dress, an example followed by the other boys.

"Humph!" murmured Hannibal Cæsar Erastus Jones, as he stood in the midst of the camp, rapidly blinking his eyes. "Fust I eber knowed a flea had a eyelash. But Massa Dick, he must know, 'case he's po'ful smart. But I 'spects I'd better git ready to serb up de grub, as dey calls it, 'case dey's allers pow'ful hungry when dey's been in swimmin'. Come t' t'ink ob it, dough, dey's most allers ready t' eat." And, chuckling to himself, Hannibal started toward the cook tent.

It did not take the boys long to dress, and as they emerged from the tents, their faces glowing with health, and bronzed from their life in the open, they were as fine a group of lads as you would meet in a day's travel, or, maybe a day and a half. They were all guests of Dick Hamilton, who, as had been his custom for several years past, had taken a crowd of his chums off to camp on the shores of Lake Dunkirk, a large body of water near Hamilton Corners, where Dick lived.

"Ah! Um! Smell that chicken!" murmured Bill Johnson, as he lifted his nose high in the air.

"There you go again! Displaying your lack of manners!" objected Fred. "Why don't you wait in patience and dignity, as I do."

"Well, wouldn't that melt your collar button!" remarked Bricktop. "Where's the glass case they took you out of, Fred?"

"Manners?" asked Dick, as he approached Fred from the side. "Excuse me, but there's something sticking out there."

As he spoke he slyly extended his foot, and, a moment later Fred measured his length on the carpet of soft, pine needles of the woods.

"Goodness me! Did you fall?" asked Dick, as he looked down, in apparent surprise at his chum. "How careless of you."

"Ha! Ha! Ha!" laughed Bill. "Come here, Fred, and I'll pick you up."

Fred arose, smiling rather sheepishly, but not at all angry. He brushed off his clothes, and joined in the laugh that followed.

"It's your turn next," observed the young millionaire. "I'll have to keep my weather eye open, Fred."

"All right," said the lad who had been tripped.

"Well, Hannibal—Alphabet—Jones; art ready for the gathering of the clans who hunger after the flesh-pots of Egypt?" asked Dick.

"All ready, Massa Dick," replied the colored cook. "Come on."

"First down! One wish-bone to gain!" called Walter Mead, as he took his place at the table set under the tent fly.

For the next five minutes the boys were so busy eating the roast chicken, corn bread and other good things that Hannibal-and-the-rest-of-it-Jones, with his knowledge of Southern cookery had provided, that they said not a word. Then, with a long-drawn sigh of satisfaction, Bill observed:

"There certainly is nothing like a good meal."

"Unless it's two," added Bricktop. "I didn't much fancy Dick's plan of taking a professional cook along when we came to camp this year, because it used to be fun to do it ourselves, but our cooking was never like this."

"Never, never, never!" exclaimed Fred. "I'll have a little more chicken, if you don't mind, Dick."

"Certainly not. There's plenty."

"Yes, this is better than having to do it ourselves," said Frank Bender, as he finished polishing off a juicy leg. "No dishes to wash, nothing to bother with after you're through, only have a good time. Dick, you're a brick!"

"As long as I'm not a gold one, it's all right," said the millionaire's son. "But I thought you'd agree with me that it was best to take a cook along."

"It sure is all to the pancake batter," observed Bricktop. "Well, I don't mind if I do have a little more of the white meat, if you insist," he added, though no one had asked him to pass his plate.

Dick laughed as he helped his chum to some choice bits. Matters were moving more slowly, now that the first edge of hunger was dulled, and the boys were taking occasional stops to make remarks.

"What's the program for this afternoon?" asked Walter, as he drained his coffee cup. "Are we going fishing?"

"Whatever you say," replied Dick, who, like a true host, always consulted the wishes of his guests. "We can fish, take a walk, or go out in the motor boat."

"The motor boat for mine," said Bill. "I want to get on a pile of cushions and take a snooze."

"Well, wouldn't that give you the nightmare!" came from Bricktop. "You're getting lazier every day, Bill."

"Help yourself," spoke the sleepy youth, as he slumped from the table and stretched out under a tree.

"I guess a trip in the motor boat would suit us all best," observed Dick. "Hannibal 'Rastus, just fill up the gasolene tank, will you?"

"Oh, why wasn't I born rich instead of handsome," murmured Bricktop, who never would have taken a prize in a beauty show. "But my fatal gift of——"

"Cut it out!" cried Walter, throwing a pine cone with such good aim, that it went right into Bricktop's open mouth.

"Oh! Ah! Ug! Blug! Chug! Hum!" spluttered the discomfitted one. "Who threw that?" he demanded, when he could speak.

Nobody answered, and, feeling in no mood to get up and chastise Walter, whose sly grin proclaimed him the culprit, Bricktop stretched out again.

"Hark! That sounds like a wagon coming," observed Fred, as he sat up, after a few minutes of silence.

"Guess it's the ice man," said Dick, for he had arranged to have a supply left at the camp. He believed in having all the comforts possible when he went into the woods.

"Doesn't rumble like an ice wagon," commented Bill.

"Sounds more like a load of steel girders," added Walter.

At this, Dick arose. He peered through the trees toward a seldom-used wagon road, which ran near the camp. He caught sight of something moving.

"It's a wagon, all right," he said, "but it isn't the ice man."

A few moments later a remarkable rig hove into sight. It consisted of a rattle-trap of a wagon, loaded with all sorts of scrap iron, and drawn by a horse that looked as if it had escaped from the bone yard. It just crawled along. On the seat was a bright-faced youth, who was doing his best to excite the animal into a speed a little better than that of a snail. He jerked on the reins, called at the horse, and cracked his whip, but all to no purpose.

"It's no use!" he exclaimed, as he looked through the trees and caught sight of Dick and his chums. "He's got the pip, or something like that."

"Why, hello, Henry," called Dick. "What brings you away off here? There's no scrap around here."

"I thought maybe you boys might have had one or two that you'd sell cheap," said the young dealer in old iron, and there was a twinkle in his eyes.

"They're all too lazy to fight, except me," observed Bricktop, "and I'm too good."

"Stow that!" commanded Fred, making a pass at his chum, who jumped back out of reach.

"Aren't you quite a way from home?" asked Dick, as he went up and shook hands with Henry Darby.

"Yes, I am. But you see I'm driving around the country, collecting old iron. This is my dull season, and I took my oldest rig, and started off day before yesterday. I'm taking it easy—have to you know, on account of my horse's health. His delicate constitution makes it necessary. There doesn't seem to be much old iron about, and I've got this far, without picking up a full load."

"Why don't you give some to your horse. Iron is good for the constitution," said Dick.

"I thought of it, but you see all the iron I have is in long pieces and sticks out all sorts of ways. If my horse swallowed any of it he'd have more fine points than he's got now. So I guess I'll keep him on grain."

"But you haven't told me why you're away off here in the woods," went on Dick. "Is there any iron about here?"

"No, not that I know of. I came to find you."

"To find me?"

"Yes. I have a telegram for you. I happened to stop in the village back there, and while I was making some inquiries in the post-office, which is also the telegraph station, a message came for you. The operator had no one he could send with it, and, as I happened to know where you were camping, I said I'd take it. He gave me a quarter for bringing it out, and so I've made some profit to-day."

"A telegram!" cried Dick. "Why didn't you say so at first? Give it here," and he held out his hand.

"I didn't want to scare you," said Henry. "I was breaking the news gently."

He handed over the yellow envelope. Dick tore it open, and, as he read the short message, he gave a start.

"No bad news I hope," remarked Walter.

"No, I guess not," replied Dick slowly. "But I've got to leave for home at once."

"Leave for home!" cried his chums.

"Yes. This is from dad. It says: 'Dear Dick. Come home as soon as you get this. Important.'"

CHAPTER II

A CHANGE IN PLANS

Following Dick's reading of the telegram there was silence among the campers. They all imagined something had happened to Mr. Hamilton, Dick's father, and they hesitated to give voice to their thoughts.

"Well, I'd offer to take you home in my chariot," said Henry Darby, with a suggestion of a smile, "only I know you'd be two days on the road. Though it might be a good thing," he added "for your father would hear us coming long before he could see us, with the way this old iron rattles. I wish some one would invent noiseless scrap iron."

"Do you—do you s'pose your father is—is hurt?" asked Walter, finally putting into words what all the others thought.

"Not a bit of it," replied Dick, stoutly. "Dad knows me well enough to say right out what he means. He wants me home, for some reason or other, but I don't know what it can be," and he looked at the telegram in a puzzled sort of way, as if the slip of paper would solve the mystery for him.

"Maybe—maybe he's lost all his money," suggested Frank "and you've got to give up the camp."

"No, I guess there's no danger of dad losing all his money so quickly," relied the young millionaire. "He had plenty when I came away, two weeks ago, and he's got so many investments that he couldn't lose it all at once, even if he tried. No, it's something else. I wonder what it is?"

"I s'pose the best way to find out, is to go and ask him, about it," suggested Henry.

"That's it," assented Dick. "I could telegraph, but he might be away from home, and wouldn't get it. I guess I'll have to leave camp, fellows."

"Then we'll go, too," said Bricktop.

"No, there's no need of that. I invited you out for three weeks, and that time isn't up yet. You might as well stay. Hannibal will cook for you, and if I can come back I will. Otherwise you stay here and enjoy yourselves."

"We won't enjoy ourselves very much if you leave," said Walter regretfully, and the others echoed his sentiment.

"Well, that's a compliment to me," declared Dick, with a smile, "but I guess you'll manage to exist. Now I wonder how I'd better go? Henry, I s'pose I could ride with you to the village, and take a train."

"I should advise you to," remarked the young iron merchant. "This nag went to sleep four times coming out, and he's snoring now. No telling what he'll do on the way back. He seems to like life in the woods. I guess he must have been a wild horse once, and he's going back to nature."

"He's not very wild now," observed Bricktop, tickling the animal with a switch. "He won't even move."

"No, it takes quite a while to get him started," said Henry. "Usually I have to begin the day before, to get him into action. No, Dick, I shouldn't advise you to ride with me."

"What's the matter with the motor boat?" asked Frank. "You can go to the village in that."

"That's so," agreed Dick. "You fellows can take me over, and bring her back. We'll do it."

"Well," remarked Henry, as he began to take in the slack of the reins, preparatory to starting the horse, "I guess I'll be going. I hope you find everything all right at home, Dick."

"I guess I will. Probably this has something to do with business matters. But, say, don't you want a bite to eat? We just finished grub, and there's a little that these cannibals didn't stow away."

"Well, I do begin to feel the need of something," said the young dealer in old iron. "The crackers and cheese I got in the village weren't very filling."

"Tie your horse, and sit down to the table. Hannibal-and-half-a-dozen-other-names will get you something. Ho! Rastus!" called Dick.

"No need to tie this horse," said Henry with grim smile. "If I did he'd imagine he was home in the stable, and go so sound to sleep that it would take two days to wake him. I'll just put some oats down in front of him, and, maybe he'll rouse up enough to eat them. That will keep him from taking naps."

The youthful iron merchant did this, and, while he was making a bountiful meal from what the colored cook set before him, Dick was preparing to start for home, wondering, meanwhile, why his father had sent for him so suddenly.

Those of you who have read the first book of this series entitled "Dick Hamilton's Fortune," will need no introduction to the millionaire youth and his chums. But you boys and girls who have not previously met him, may desire a little introduction.

Dick Hamilton was the only son of Mortimer Hamilton, of Hamilton Corners, not far from New York. The town was named after Mr. Hamilton because he was financially interested in many of the industries of the place. He was president of the national bank, owned large woolen mills, a brass foundry, a lumber concern, and was head of a railroad and a trolley line that added much of importance to the place. Mr. Hamilton counted his fortune by the millions, and his son, who had inherited a large sum from his mother, was also the possessor of substantial bank accounts.

In the first volume there was told how, on a certain birthday Dick came into control of a large part of his wealth, subject to a peculiar condition of his mother's will. That is, he was to make, inside of a year, a wise and paying investment of some of his funds, under penalty of losing control of his fortune for a time, and having to live with a miserly uncle.

This uncle, Ezra Larabee by name, of the town of Dankville, was Mrs. Hamilton's brother. One of the conditions of her will was that Dick should spend a week with his uncle before entering into possession of the money, that he might see what sort of a life he was likely to lead, in case he did not comply with the provisions.

Dick had a miserable time at Mr. Larabee's. He was not allowed to have any fun, and his uncle even objected to him walking on the paths, for fear he would disturb the newly-raked gravel.

Dick returned home, determined to make a paying investment if only to escape his uncle's clutches. He did make several investments, by buying real estate, some stock in a milk company, and some shares in a gold mine. But they all turned out badly, and, while investigating the mine by means of which he had been swindled, he had, with his chums, some exciting adventures.

In Hamilton Corners, dwelt "Hank" Darby, a shiftless sort of man, and his son, Henry, who was as energetic as his father was lazy. Henry started to make money, in a small way, by collecting scrap iron, and selling it, but his shiftless parent nearly brought the business to grief. Dick became interested in Henry's efforts, and, as the young millionaire had plenty of money, he loaned Henry two hundred and fifty dollars, to buy out the iron business of a man who wished to retire. "Hank" Darby, with an exaggerated idea of his own importance, elected himself president of the old iron company, made Dick treasurer, and Henry secretary.

Dick gave little thought to the money he had loaned his young friend, but the time came when it was to prove of great benefit to him. One after another his various investments failed, and he saw the time approaching when he must go to live with his miserly uncle. His last venture was to invest five hundred dollars in an airship, the inventor of which hoped to win a government prize, which he promised to divide with Dick. But the airship blew up, and Dick saw his next birthday dawn, without, as he thought, having made his paying investment.

Uncle Ezra, who was much opposed to his nephew having so much money, came, according to agreement, to get Dick to take him to Dankville with him. But, at the last moment, something quite unexpected happened and it was found that Dick had, after all, complied with the terms of his mother's will, and he was, therefore, allowed to keep control of his fortune. But, as told in the first volume, there were still other stipulations with which he must comply.

Following the events told of in "Dick Hamilton's Fortune," our millionaire hero had completed his course at a local academy. When summer came he took some of his chums off to camp in the woods, and it was there that Henry, who was still in the old iron business, found him.

"Well, I guess I'm ready," remarked Dick, as he came from his tent, one of several that formed the camp. "I'll not take any of my things, for I may be able to come back and finish out the vacation."

"I certainly hope so," said Bricktop fervently.

"Same here," added Walter and the others.

By this time Henry had made a good meal, and, as his horse showed some signs of life, he remarked that he thought he would start, before the beast got to sleep again.

"Did you gasolene the motor boat, Rastus?" asked Dick of the colored cook.

"Yais sah, Massa Dick."

"All right. Now see that these poor kids don't get hungry while I'm gone. Let 'em take pieces of pie to bed with 'em, to keep 'em quiet."

"Ho! Ho! Massa Dick. Deed an' I will. Pie to bed wif 'em! Ha! Ha! Ho! Ho!"

The boys entered the motor boat, leaving Hannibal in charge of camp, and they soon reached the village, whence Dick could take a train for home.

"Now, fellows, enjoy yourselves," he called to them, as they watched him board the train at the depot. "I'll come back if I can. Better practice that triple summersault, Frank."

"I will. I'll stump you, when you come back."

"I wish I didn't have to leave them," thought Dick, as he settled himself in his seat. "I wonder what dad wants of me? But there's no use worrying. I'll be home in about two hours."

He exhibited his pass, on which he was traveling, as his father was president of the railroad, and then sat looking at the scenery, vainly wondering, in spite of his efforts not to dwell on it, why he had been summoned home.

"Well, Dick," greeted his father, when the young millionaire entered the house. "You got back sooner than I expected."

"Yes, dad. I started as soon as I got your message. I hope nothing is the matter."

"Nothing serious. The fact is I have to leave for Europe next week——"

"For Europe! And are you going to take me?"

"No, I'm sorry to say I can't. But I have other plans for you, which I hope you will like. I unexpectedly received a call to England, to settle some large financial matters in which I am interested, and, as I shall have to be gone six months or more I decided to close the house up and let the servants go. As that would make no place for you to stay, unless you boarded, which you might not like, I decided to send for you, and tell you what I propose. The reason I telegraphed for you is that I will be so busy after to-day that I will have no time to attend to anything."

"What are you going to do with me?" asked Dick.

"You remember," went on Mr. Hamilton, "that in her will, your mother specified, in addition to making a good investment, that you must attend a military academy——"

"That's so!" cried Dick. "I'd forgotten about that. Say, when can I go? This beats camp!"

"Not so fast," cautioned his father. "There are certain conditions to be fulfilled. Your mother had peculiar ideas regarding money. She wished her son to become a success in spite of it. So she provided, under certain penalties, which you will learn of later, that you were to go to a good military academy to complete your education.

"There, as I told you once before, though you may have forgotten it, you are to become popular with the students in spite of your wealth. You are to make your own way without the aid of your millions. And this is no easy matter. While many persons have a false notion of wealth, by far the larger class attach to it only the importance it deserves. A rich lad can, to a certain extent, become popular, but he will never have the real, solid friends that some youth not so well off would win. So you've got to make friends in spite of your money."

"That ought to be easy," said Dick, but he was to find it a harder task than he had supposed it would be.

"So, as I have to go away, and close up the house," went on Mr. Hamilton, "I have arranged that you are to go to the academy a little ahead of time, about two weeks before the term opens. That will give you a chance to find your way around the place."

"Where is it?"

"It is the Kentfield Military Academy, located in one of the middle western states, and is near Lake Wagatook. Colonel James Masterly, a friend of mine, is the superintendent, and I have written to him concerning you. He gave me permission to send you on ahead of time, and that is what I propose to do. You will have to get ready to go at the end of this week. I hope you do not object."

"Not in the least, dad. We were having lots of fun at camp, but I'll have more fun at Kentfield. Shoulder arms! present arms! Halt! parade rest! Wow! Say, dad, this is the best yet!"

"Wait until you've spent a term there," advised his father.

"If I don't have to start until the end of the week, I might as well go back to camp," said Dick, when he had calmed down a bit.

"Just as you like. From now on I shall be too busy to see much of you, but I will make all arrangements."

"All right, dad. I'll go back to camp then. I can get a late train," and Dick went to see what time it left, meanwhile whistling a succession of military airs, from "The Girl I left Behind Me," to "Yankee Doodle."

He reached camp late that night, somewhat to the surprise of his chums, and they spent the next few days in crowding in as much pleasure as possible. When it became time for Dick to leave, the others decided to go back home with him, as the three weeks were nearly up.

CHAPTER III

GRIT ROUTS UNCLE EZRA

"There's a man out in the vestibule who wants to see you, Master Dick," said Gibbs, the butler, one evening, a few days before the time of departure to the academy.

"Who is it?"

"Captain Handlee."

"Tell him to come in." Dick knew Captain Handlee as an old soldier, who lived in a tumble-down house on the outskirts of the village. The veteran, escorted by the butler, entered shyly. Dick greeted him kindly, and the old man began almost abruptly:

"Did you ever hear that I had a son?"

"No, I never knew that. Where is he?"

"That is what I want you to help me to find out."

"You want me to help you? Why, how can I?" asked Dick.

"I don't know that you can. I only hope so. Will you?"

"I will do all I can for you, but perhaps you want to see my father," for Dick had an idea that the old man wanted some money for some purpose.

"No, I want to see you, Mr. Dick. You see you are going to a military academy, and that is why I think you can help me."

"But I don't understand."

"Listen, and I will tell you. As you know, I am an old soldier, but few persons around here know that my only son was a soldier, too."

"I certainly did not. I never knew that you had a son."

"Well, I did, and he was a fine chap, too. He enlisted in the regular army, where I served my time, but for many years I have heard nothing about him."

"What happened?"

"He was among the missing after his company was sent to quell an uprising among the Indians, out west, many years ago. No word was ever received from him, and I don't know whether he was killed, or taken captive. I never heard anything about him, and now I think you can aid me in locating him."

"But how can I?"

"By making inquiries at the military academy."

"But it is not likely that any one at Kentfield would know of your son."

"They might. When your father told me you were going there, he mentioned that Major Franklin Webster, a retired army officer, was in charge of military tactics at the school. Now Major Webster is an old Indian fighter, and I thought that if you asked him, he might be able to get some news of my son. Will you do this for me?"

"I will, gladly, but I have not much hope of the result."

"Perhaps it will amount to nothing," said the old soldier with a sigh, "but it is the first chance I have had in many years. All my inquiries of the war department resulted in nothing. Perhaps you may have better luck."

"I hope so," replied Dick gently. "I will make some inquiries. What is your son's name?"

"He was christened William, but his friends in the army called him Corporal Bill."

"How would Major Webster know him?"

"Oh, easily enough. I have his picture."

The veteran drew a faded photograph from his pocket, and held the card so that Dick could see it. "That's him," said the old man proudly.

The young millionaire saw the photograph of a youthful soldier in uniform.

"Your son would be much older than that now; wouldn't he, Captain Handlee?"

"Yes, I suppose so. I think he must have been injured in some way, and forgotten his name. Otherwise he would have written to me. But I know another way in which you could recognize him."

"How?"

"He was the best shot in his company. He was a sharpshooter, and one of the finest. So if you can get track of a soldier, who is a good shot, that may be my son, Corporal Bill. Will you try?"

"I will, Captain, I'll do my best."

"God bless you," said the veteran fervently. "And now I'll leave you. I'd let you take this photograph, only it's—it's all I have to remember—my son by," and his voice choked.

"I don't believe I'll need that," answered Dick. "I'll speak to Major Webster, and see what I can do."

The old soldier, murmuring his thanks, left the house.

"Well," mused Dick, as he went to his room, "I'll soon be at Kentfield. It'll be lonesome, at first, I expect, but the cadets will soon arrive. And I'll try to find the captain's son.

"I wonder how I'll make out with the cadets? I don't see why I should have any trouble making friends, or becoming popular, no matter if I am a millionaire, and the son of one. Money ought not to make such a difference. Still, as dad says, I may find it a handicap."

He looked around the room where he had spent so many pleasant hours. It was an ideal boy's apartment, with everything the most exacting youth could desire.

"I think I'll make out all right," Dick mused on. "But if worst comes to worst, I have a plan up my sleeve which I think will work." His eyes sparkled, and it was evident that he had just thought of some scheme. "That ought to do it," he said, speaking half aloud. "If I can't win any other way, I'll try that."

"Well, Dick," remarked his father, the next morning, "I suppose you are all ready to go to Kentfield?"

"Yes. I've got everything packed. What will be your address on the other side?"

"Oh, yes, I must leave you that. Here it is. You can forward me letters in care of my London bankers, and they will see that I get them. I may have to put in some time on the continent. By the way, Dick, I hear that Captain Handlee called to see you last night."

"Yes, he wants me to help him locate his missing son," and Dick told his father of the interview with the old soldier.

"Poor man," remarked Mr. Hamilton, shaking his head, "I fear there is little hope for him. I once aided him in making some inquiries, but they came to nothing."

"Do you know him?"

"Oh, yes, I have often aided him, and I would do more for him, but he is too proud to accept charity. He is rather odd at times, and does not remain at any employment long, or I could give him a good place. His whole mind is set on finding his son. If the missing corporal could be located it would be the making of Captain Handlee, for he would settle down then."

"I don't suppose I can help him."

"No, I'm afraid not. Still, do all you can. It is barely possible that Major Webster, or some of the officers who are stationed at Kentfield, may be able to put you on the track, but I doubt it. Well, I think I'll have to go down to the bank now. I'll see you to-night, and say good-bye in the morning."

Not long after Mr. Hamilton had left, and while Dick was in his room, packing some of his belongings, a maid who was new in the house came to inform him that a visitor was in the library.

"Who is it?" he asked.

"I don't know, but it's someone, Master Dick, who your dog doesn't like, for he's growling something fierce."

"I'll come down," said the young millionaire, and he hurried to the library. As he entered a tall, thin man, with a curious little bunch of whiskers on his chin, arose.

"Well, I must say, Nephew Richard," he began, in a rasping voice, "that this is a nice reception for me. Your horrible beast nearly bit me. The house is no place for dogs."

"I'm sorry that Grit annoyed you, Uncle Ezra," said Dick as he recognized the miserly man whom he had once visited.

"Hum!" grunted the old man. "If I hadn't stood on a chair he would have bit me, and then I'd get hydrophobia, and die. Your father would have had to pay damages, too."

"I'm glad no such thing as that happened, Uncle Ezra."

"Hum! Where's your father?"

"Down to the bank. I can telephone, and let him know that you are here."

"It isn't necessary. No need of wearing out the wires that way. I can wait. I hear he has some foolish notion of sending you to a military school."

"I am going to a military academy, Uncle Ezra, in accordance with my mother's wishes."

"Stuff and nonsense! A wicked waste of money! The ordinary schools were good enough for me, and they ought to be good enough for you. It's a sinful waste of money. Mortimer Hamilton ought to be ashamed of himself. The money ought to go to the heathen. It's foolish."

"My father doesn't think so," replied Dick as quietly as he could, though he was fast becoming angry at the dictatorial tone of his crabbed uncle.

"Hum! Much he knows about it! The idea of putting such ideas into boys' heads as fighting and killing. Hu!"

"But it might be useful in case of war."

"Stuff and nonsense! It's positively wicked, I tell you. I've come to remonstrate with Mortimer about it. If he has to go to Europe, which is another waste of money, he could leave you with me. I'd bring you up in the way you should go. There's no nonsense about me, nor my wife, either. If your father consents to having you come to my place, you'll learn more than you would at any military academy. Stuff and nonsense! Don't talk to me! I know!"

Dick could not repress a shudder as he thought of his uncle's gloomy home in Dankville, a house amid a clump of fir trees, so dark, so quiet and so lonesome that it reminded him of a vault in the cemetery.

"I think my father has made up his mind to send me to the military academy," said the boy.

"Well, perhaps I can make him change his mind. He doesn't know what's good for boys."

How Uncle Ezra Larabee could understand what lads needed, never having had any sons of his own, was more than Dick could fathom, but he said nothing.

"I'll wait and see your father," went on the crabbed man.

"I can get my automobile and take you to the bank," suggested Dick.

"No, you might burst a tire, and that would cost something to fix."

Dick could hardly repress a smile at the idea of a possible injured tire standing in the way of an auto ride.

"What's that girl walking back and forth so much for in the next room?" asked Uncle Ezra suddenly.

"That's the maid, clearing away the breakfast things."

"Hum! She'll wear the carpet out," commented the old man. "I must speak to Mortimer about it. I think I'll caution her now."

He rose, to do this, but accidentally stepped on one of Grit's legs, as the animal was reposing under a chair, where Dick had sent him to get him out of the way. The dog let out a howl, and then a savage growl, and made for the man he felt had purposely injured him.

"Hold him! Catch him!" cried Uncle Ezra, as he sprang away. "Hold him, Nephew Richard!"

"Grit!" called Dick. "Come here!"

But the dog refused to mind. Growling and snarling, he ran after Uncle Ezra. The latter did not stop to speak to the maid about wearing out the carpet. Instead he kept on to the front hall, and to the entrance door, which was, fortunately, open. Down the steps, three at a time, jumped Mr. Larabee, the dog close behind him.

But, by this time Dick had caught up to his pet, and grasped him by the collar.

"Grit! Aren't you ashamed of yourself?" he asked, but he could hardly keep from smiling, while, as for Grit, he nearly wagged off his stump of a tail, so glad was he at having routed Uncle Ezra.

"I'll go down and see your father at the bank!" cried the excited man, turning when he was safely on the sidewalk. "The idea of having a savage beast like that in the house. I'll see Mortimer and make him change his plans. And I tell you one thing, Nephew Richard, if you come to live with me you'll have to get rid of that bulldog," and, angrily shaking his head, Uncle Ezra tramped down the street, walking slowly to save shoe leather, though he was a very rich man.

"I hope dad doesn't allow himself to be influenced by Uncle Ezra," thought Dick, as he went back into the house with the dog. "We never could stand it at Dankville; could we, Grit?" And the animal whined as if he understood.

CHAPTER IV

IN WHICH DICK STARTS OFF

Mr. Hamilton came home early that afternoon, bringing Mr. Larabee, his brother-in-law, with him. Dick was anxiously awaiting their arrival.

"Is that fierce beast in the house?" demanded the boy's uncle, as he stood on the front steps. "If he is I'll not come in."

"I've sent him to the stable, uncle," replied the young millionaire.

"That's the proper place for him. Dogs are no good. They eat as much as a man, and what you spend on keeping them would provide for a heathen child in Africa."

Dick wondered if Uncle Ezra provided for any heathen children, from his wealth, but did not think it wise to ask.

"Well, Dick," said Mr. Hamilton, when they were all three in the library, "your uncle thinks it would be a good plan for me to leave you with him, while I'm away."

"Yes?" remarked Dick, his heart beating faster than usual.

"It's the only sensible plan," said Uncle Ezra with a snort. "Your idea of a military academy, where he'll learn to shoot and stab his fellow citizens, is a foolish one, Mortimer."

"It is not altogether my plan," said Mr. Hamilton softly as he thought of his dead wife. "Dick's mother provided for his future in her will, and I must see that her wishes are carried out. Besides, I think a military training is good for a young man."

"Stuff and nonsense!" exclaimed Uncle Ezra. "Neither you nor I had it, Mortimer, and we got along. We're both well off."

"Money isn't everything," said Mr. Hamilton. "No, Ezra, I'm much obliged for your offer, but I think Dick will go to Kentfield. He is to start in the morning."

"Hum! It's a foolish idea," again snorted Uncle Ezra. "You'll live to see the day you'll both be sorry for it."

"I hope not, Ezra."

"Well, you will."

"We'll not discuss that now. Will you have a cigar before dinner?"

"I never smoke. It's a dangerous and expensive habit."

"Slightly dangerous, perhaps, but I smoke very little. As for the expense, I think I can afford it. This has been quite a prosperous year for me—and Dick."

"What you spend for cigars would pay the interest on a large loan," went on Mr. Larabee.

"Yes, but I don't need the loan," declared Mr. Hamilton with a smile, "and I do feel that I need a cigar to rest me after my day's work. However, I don't advocate tobacco for young men, and Dick has promised not to smoke until he is of age, and that will not be for a few years yet."

"Stuff and nonsense!" exclaimed Uncle Ezra, as he could thing of nothing else to say.

"Perhaps you'd like a glass of lemonade before dinner," suggested Dick.

"No," replied the austere man. "I don't think I'll stop for dinner. My visit here has resulted in no good, and the sooner I get back home the better. Besides I've got a new hired man, and I'm almost certain he'll set the barn afire; he's so careless."

"Oh, I hope not, Ezra," said Mr. Hamilton.

"So do I, but I'd be nervous all night and I wouldn't sleep. Then I might get sick, and have to pay out money for a doctor, or some medicine. No; I'll take the late train home."

"But that won't get you there until after midnight."

"That's all right. It'll be cooler then, and there won't be so much danger of overheating the horse. When you overheat a horse you sometimes have to buy medicine for him, and horse medicine is expensive."

Seeing that his brother-in-law could not be prevailed upon to remain, Mr. Hamilton bade him good-bye, and Dick offered to take his uncle to the depot in the auto, but Mr. Larabee would not hear of it. He would walk, he said, and save the car fare.

"He's a queer man—your uncle," said Mr. Hamilton that night. "I guess you wouldn't fancy staying with him; eh Dick?"

"No, indeed, dad. A military academy for mine, as Bricktop would say."

Dick was up early the next morning, when both he and his father were to go away from home, each for a considerable time. The servants had been provided for, and the handsome Hamilton mansion would be closed for several months. Dick accompanied his father to the bank after breakfast, and planned to go to the depot from there, some of his chums having arranged to meet him at the station.

"Ah, good morning, gentlemen!" exclaimed a pompous voice, as Dick and his father entered the institution, and the young millionaire saw "Hank" Darby, ready to greet them. "I understand you are about to become a soldier," he went on to Dick.

"Well, a sort of one," replied our hero.

"Ah, that's a grand and noble calling. I once thought I would be one of the defenders of my country, but I was called into other lines of activity," said the father of the young proprietor of the scrap iron business. He did not specify what the other lines were. "It is indeed noble to fight for one's flag," went on the shiftless man, "but it is also noble to accumulate wealth with which to fit out armies. That is what I am doing. I am accumulating wealth."

"How is it going?" asked Mr. Hamilton, who, as well as did Dick, knew that Henry, the son, made all the money, which "Hank" spent as fast as he could get any of it.

"Well, it might be better," said the shiftless one. "But I have a scheme on hand."

"Another scheme, eh?"

"Yes, this is a very good one. There are enormous possibilities in it, sir, *enormous*!" and "Hank" fairly stood on his tiptoes to get this last word out with much emphasis.

"Well, I hope you succeed," said Mr. Hamilton, as he and his son went to the millionaire's private office.

The final details for the trips of father and son were arranged. Dick had his own bank account, and would not want for money. His father gave him some advice, and then the two said good-bye to each other, Dick having to leave before his father did, as the latter was to take an express to New York, where he would get a steamer for Europe. Grit, the dog, was to be left in charge of Henry Darby.

"Well, my boy," said Mr. Hamilton, as he shook hands with Dick, "remember what you are going for. You're under a big handicap, but I guess you will win. You did the other time, though it was a close shave."

"Good-bye," said Dick, unable to keep back the suspicion of a tear.

"Good-bye," replied Mr. Hamilton, turning hastily to his desk, and fumbling among some papers, which seemed to rattle unnecessarily loud.

On the way to the depot Dick met Captain Handlee. The veteran greeted the lad cordially.

"So you're off to learn to be a soldier?" he asked.

"Well, I don't know that the military part of it amounts to much," admitted Dick, who had no false ideas about where he was going, "but dad thinks the discipline will be good for me, I guess."

"That's right. Nothing like discipline of the right sort for lads. We didn't have to learn to be soldiers in my time."

"No, I s'pose you just went right in and fought," said Dick.

"Indeed we did. That's what my boy did. Poor Bill! I wish I could see him, or even hear of him again. You'll not forget your promise; will you?"

"No, Captain Handlee."

"Remember he was the best shot in his company. He could drive a tack in a board at a hundred yards. You make some inquiries, and I think you'll get on the track of him."

"I will," promised Dick, but he had no idea in what a strange way fate was to bring about the old captain's desires through him.

Dick found a crowd of his chums awaiting for him at the railroad station.

"Here he comes!" cried Frank Bender, as he caught sight of Dick.

"Aren't you going to take your rifle with you?" asked Fred Murdock.

"I guess they'll provide me with a gun at Kentfield," answered Dick.

"But they won't give you such grub as we had at camp," remarked Bricktop.

"Oh, I guess they will, but maybe it won't taste so good," replied the young millionaire. "Well, boys, I guess this is my train."

All his chums tried to shake hands with Dick at once as the locomotive pulled into the station.

"Don't forget to send me a souvenier postal," called Bill Johnson.

"Tell us how you like it," chimed in Walter.

"Maybe my dad will send me," added Bricktop.

"Tell us if you meet any girls as pretty as those here," was Fred's contribution.

"Get on the football team," advised Frank.

"And the baseball nine," chimed in Bricktop.

By this time a number of passengers had their heads out of the windows, to see who was getting such a send-off. Dick's chums shook him by the hand, clapped him on the back, and fairly carried him up the steps of the coach.

Then, amid a chorus of good-byes, the train pulled out, and Dick was started on his way to become a cadet.

CHAPTER V

AN ODD CHARACTER

It was evening when Dick arrived at Kentfield, which, from the scenes about the station, he judged to be quite a town of little importance. There were few signs of life, scarcely anyone being at the depot, and only a few passengers alighting.

"I wonder if I can get a carriage to take me out to the academy?" mused Dick, as he looked about. "This doesn't strike me as being much of a place, but the catalogue dad got showed quite an academy. I wonder where it is?"

He saw a rather dilapidated hack standing near the platform, and, walking up to it, addressed the driver.

"Can you take me out to the military academy?" he asked.

"Sure," replied the man, "but there's nothing to see. It isn't open yet. Term doesn't begin until next week."

"I know," replied Dick. "But I'm going to attend there."

"You?"

The man seemed much surprised, but there was a noticeable change in his manner.

"Going to be a student there?" he asked respectfully.

"Yes. I had to come on ahead of time."

"All right. Take you out there in a jiffy," went on the hack driver briskly. "Got any baggage?"

Dick handed over his checks, and the man soon returned with his trunk and suitcase.

"This doesn't appear to be a very lively place; not as much so as I expected," remarked the young millionaire as he got into the vehicle.

"Oh, bless your heart, sir, you just wait until next week," said the man. "Then this town will sit up and take notice. This is our off season, when the military school is closed. But when the boys arrive—wow! Say, then's when you got to look out. My! Oh my! But it's fierce!"

"Do they—do they cut up much?" asked Dick, secretly glad that he was to have a hand in it if the students did.

"Do they? Say, young man, when I start to drive a party of them cadets anywhere I don't never know if we're going to arrive. Never can tell when a wheel is coming off, or when my horses will start up, and leave the coach behind. That's why I always use quiet animals. Them cadets has life enough and to spare. Cut up? Say, jest you wait!"

"Well, maybe it won't be so bad after I get started, and make the acquaintance of some of the boys," thought Dick.

But he little knew what was ahead of him.

"Is the academy far out?" asked Dick, for, as the hack was an open one, he could converse with the driver.

"About a mile. We'll be there in a jiffy."

A "jiffy" must be quite a period of time, or else the driver's estimate of a mile was different from the accepted five thousand two hundred and eighty feet, for dusk changed to darkness before the hackman turned in between two big, stone pillars, and the man announced:

"Here we are."

"I don't see anything," objected Dick.

"It's too dark. But the buildings are right ahead of you."

Then the lad was able to make out the dim forms of a number of structures located in a sort of park.

"Where's the lake?" asked Dick. "I thought the academy was on a lake."

"So it is. That's on the other side. We're sort of coming in from the back, but that's the shortest road from the depot. I'll take you right to Colonel Masterly's quarters. He's the one you want to see, I guess, being as you're a new cadet, and he's the superintendent."

"I suppose so," answered Dick.

A little later he alighted in front of a large brick structure, and the hackman lifted down his trunk and suitcase.

"Do they expect you?" asked the driver.

"I think so," replied our hero, hoping that some arrangements had been made for him.

A moment later a door opened, and a flood of light streamed out from a broad hall. A man in semi-military uniform appeared.

"Who's there?" he asked, and, having spoken he began to whistle a few bars from "Marching Through Georgia," ending up with a bugle call.

"Got a cadet for you, Toots," replied the hackman.

"A cadet?" and once more the man in the hall whistled a martial air.

"That's what I said, Toots. Give me a hand with this trunk, will you, and tell Colonel Masterly that he's going to have company."

"My name's Hamilton," began Dick. "I believe my father arranged——"

"Oh yes, the colonel told me to look out for you," said the man who looked like a soldier. "Come right in. The colonel will be here directly. I'll take your baggage."

"Thank you—er Mr.——" and Dick hesitated, for he did not just know how to address the person in the hall, and wanted to make no mistake in bestowing a military title.

"Me? Oh I'm Sam Sander," said the man in the blue suit, apparently surprised that his identity was not known.

"Yes, that's Sam," went on the hack driver, with easy familiarity, "but nobody calls him that; do they, Toots?"

The other, who was helping to carry in Dick's trunk did not answer. Instead he whistled the bugle call for "Taps," or lights out.

"Do they, Toots?" repeated the hack driver.

"Do they what?" inquired the soldier, who seemed to be rather absent minded.

"Do they call you anything but Toots?"

"Nope. That's what they call me. I don't mind. I've almost forgotten what my real name is. Toots is good enough I expect."

"He's a queer chap," whispered the hackman to Dick, as our hero paid him. "Queer, but all right. He's a sort of general helper around the grounds. Well, good night. I'll see you again maybe, when some of the other lads begin to arrive. And then won't there be lively times! Wow! My! Oh my! But them students certainly know how to have fun!"

The hackman appeared to relish the prospect, and Dick could hear him chuckling to himself as he drove off in the darkness.

"Right this way, Mr. Hamilton," said Toots, which name we shall adopt for him. "I will find the colonel for you——"

He stopped suddenly, straightened up, in spite of the suitcase which he was carrying, and gave a stiff military salute.

"Mr. Hamilton has arrived, sir," he said, and at that Dick caught sight of a tall thin man, with an iron gray moustache and imperial, coming down the broad, well-lighted hall.

"Ah, Hamilton, glad to see you," said the soldierly-looking gentleman, extending his hand. "I'm Colonel Masterly. You are a little early, but I understand the case. Have you had dinner?"

Dick had not, and said so.

"Then you can dine with me," went on Colonel Masterly. "Sam, take Mr. Hamilton's baggage to the room I told you to get ready for him. I'll quarter you here for the present," he added, "until the boys arrive, and then you will have a roommate. How is your father?"

"Quite well," replied Dick, and then he followed the superintendent into a reception room. There two other military-looking men sat reading books. They looked up at the entrance of Dick and the colonel, who introduced them to the new student as Major Henry Rockford, commandant of the academy, and Major Franklin Webster, U. S. A., retired, who was in charge of military tactics at the school.

"That's the man of whom I must inquire about Captain Handlee's missing son," thought Dick, as the two instructors shook hands with him. "But I guess I'll wait a few days."

Dinner was rather a formal affair, and our hero did not in the least enjoy it. The three men talked of matters connected with the prospective opening of the school, occasionally addressing a question to Dick, or making some general remark.

The academy more than came up to Dick's expectations when he saw it the next morning. The school was made up of several buildings, consisting of a main barracks, which was where he had spent the night, and which contained the executive offices and class rooms, two other barracks, a gymnasium, a large mess hall, a riding hall, a small hospital and other structures.

They were grouped on a large plain, that lay at the foot of quite a mountain range, but, what pleased Dick more than anything else, was a large lake that came right to the edge of the academy grounds. It was a beautiful sheet of water, and, from the appearance of a large boathouse near at hand, Dick guessed rightly that the cadet-students spent considerable time rowing and sailing.

After breakfast, under the guidance of Toots, who was detailed by Colonel Masterly for that purpose, Dick was taken on a tour of the grounds. He was particularly pleased with the big stable, which contained a fine lot of horses.

"Are those for the cadets to use?" he asked Toots.

"Of course. Do you know how to ride?"

"A little," replied Dick, who did not believe in boasting, though, in reality, he was a fine horseman.

"I'll certainly have a swell time here," he thought, as he strolled about. He obtained permission to row out on the lake, and then was left to his own resources.

After the first novelty of seeing the buildings had worn off, Dick began to feel a little lonesome, and he wished that the week was up, and that the other students would begin to arrive. But he found much to interest him, and made friends with Toots, who told him many and various stories of student life.

"Why do they call you Toots?" asked Dick one day.

"Well, I s'pose it's because I've got in the habit of tooting my whistle all the while. I'm always whistling war tunes or bugle calls, the boys say."

"That's so. What makes you?"

"I don't know, except that I'm fond of a military life. Some day I'm going to war."

"Well, I hope you don't get shot," said Dick, as Toots left him, still whistling.

It was a few days after this that Dick saw a new student arrive. The lad, for reasons similar to those affecting our hero, had been sent to the academy in advance of the opening of the term. Dick soon made his acquaintance, and he found the newcomer rather an odd character. His name was William Schoop, but he was called "William the Silent" by the other cadets, so Major Webster said, from the fact that he did not talk much. He used only single words where others would take a sentence, and he often made gestures answer for words.

Dick and Will soon became friends, and the latter, who had spent a previous term at the school, showed the young millionaire about the buildings and grounds.

CHAPTER VI

THE HAZING

One morning, two days after the arrival of the silent lad, when Dick had moved his baggage to his permanent room in the south barracks, the two lads were strolling about the campus. Dick was beginning to wish his companion was more sociable, when Will, with a sudden gesture, pointed off toward the town, along the main road that led from the station. Dick looked, and saw a cloud of dust approaching.

"What's that?" he inquired.

"Fellows coming," was all Will replied.

He started off toward the main gate, and Dick followed. The dust clouds became larger, and approached closer. Then Dick saw that they were made by two large stages, and, a little later, he could discern that the vehicles were crowded with youths.

Above the rumble of the wheels could be heard laughing, joyous voices. There were shouts, yells, cheers, whoops and cries.

"Three cheers for Kentfield!" called some one, and the resulting yells caused the horses of the stage to prance more madly than ever.

A few moments later the vehicles had halted at the gate, and from them, pell-mell leaped the cadets, returning to the academy after the long, summer vacation.

"There's William the Silent!" cried one lad, rushing up to Dick's odd friend, and shaking hands with him. "Hello, Will! How are you? Are you the only one here, so far?"

William merely nodded. Then he waved his hand toward our hero.

"Dick Hamilton," he said.

Dick stepped forward to greet the students, expecting them to tell him their names. From the group of cadets that had gathered around Will, a tall, good looking chap, but with rather a hard, cruel gleam in his dark eyes, stepped forth.

"What's your name, new chap?" he asked somewhat sneeringly.

"Hamilton—Dick Hamilton," replied the young millionaire.

"Oh, Hamilton—Millionaire Hamilton's son, eh?" asked Dick's questioner, with an unpleasant air.

"I believe so," answered Dick, trying to smile good-naturedly in spite of the overbearing air of the lad, who was no older than himself.

"I've heard about you," went on the other. "Fellows," he said, turning to those surrounding him, "this is the young hostage of fortune who has consented to dwell a while in our midst. I saw a little paragraph in the paper a few days ago to the effect that Millionaire Hamilton's son had decided to take a course at Kentfield Military Academy. That is he condescended to inflict his presence on us. I'm sure the academy is highly honored," and the lad made a mocking bow.

Dick felt the hot flush rising to his face. He had never been so insulted before. An angry reply was on his lips.

"Millions don't go here, Hamilton," said another youth. "Your money won't count, and the sooner you find that out the better. Come on, fellows, let's see if old Toots is still alive, and then we'll have some fun."

"Ta-ta, Hamilton, I suppose you brought a solid gold bedstead with you," said the lad who had first spoken, as he turned on his heel, and followed the others. "Maybe you'd like to buy the place," he fired back over his shoulder.

"You—you——" began Dick angrily.

He was stopped by a touch on his shoulder. He looked around, to see William the Silent standing near him.

"Take it easy," was all Will said, but Dick understood.

Choking down, as best he could, his righteous wrath at the mean treatment accorded him, Dick strolled down to the lake. Will did not attempt to follow, for he understood.

Sorely puzzled over the conduct of those whom he hoped would be his friends, Dick got into a boat, and went out for a solitary row. He wanted to be alone and think.

"It's queer they should treat me that way," he mused. "I'm sure I don't make any fuss about my money. Maybe they are afraid I'll try to, and they're taking no chances. But they ought to give a fellow a show first."

After rowing about for an hour Dick felt better. He resolved not to force his friendship on the students, but to let matters take their course. He had expected a little "stand-offishness" on the part of the older cadets, who were always, more or less, inclined to be on their dignity with freshmen.

"Well, I'll wait until some new fellows arrive," thought Dick. "I guess I can make friends with them."

When he returned to shore he found that many more students had come in, the next day marking the opening of the term. Among the lads were a number of new cadets, as Dick could easily tell by their bashful, diffident manners. He felt that he had somewhat the advantage of them, for he had been at the place more than a week.

"Still, my only acquaintances, outside of the teachers are William the Silent, Toots and the hostler," he reflected.

There was a notice posted on the campus bulletin board to the effect that all new students were to report at the south barrack. Thither Dick went, finding Captain Hayden, the head master in charge, showing the boys to their rooms.

"Ah, Hamilton," called the captain, as he caught sight of Dick, "you are to room with Paul Drew, on the second floor. Room Twenty-six is yours. I think you can find your way there. Go up and take Drew with you."

A tall quiet youth greeted Dick with a smile.

"I'm Drew," he said. "I suppose you're Hamilton?"

"What there is of me," answered the millionaire youth. "Is this your first term?"

He knew it was, but he wanted to say something.

"Yes. I'm from Kentucky."

"I'm a York Stater. Come on and I'll show you where we bunk."

The two made their way through crowds of new boys and were soon in their apartment.

It was like all the others provided for the use of the students. It contained two small iron beds, and was simply furnished.

"Here's where we'll be at home," observed Dick. "Have you any choice as to a bed?"

"No, either one will suit me."

"All right, we'll toss up for it. Heads is the one nearest the window. You call."

Dick spun a coin in the air.

"Tails!" cried young Drew.

"Tails it is," announced Dick.

"Then I'll take the bed away from the window. It's likely to be cold in the winter."

"I don't mind. I like a cool breeze now and then. But stow away your things and come on down. There's lots to see. I hope we get into our uniforms soon. You've got yours, haven't you?"

"Yes," replied Dick's roommate. Dick had been provided with the necessary dress uniform before leaving home, and he was anxious to don it. The other uniforms were to be obtained at the academy.

The two boys, after hastily putting away their things, went down on the campus, which was fairly swarming with old and new students. More boys were arriving with every stage, and the shouts and cries, as former acquaintances greeted one another, made the green sound like an athletic ground with a championship match in progress.

As Dick and Paul stood looking about them, the young millionaire felt some one touch him on the arm. He turned and saw William Schoop. Will nodded his head to indicate that he wanted Dick to step aside for a moment. Excusing himself from his roommate Dick walked a little distance, following William the Silent.

"Don't mind Dutton," said William.

"Who's Dutton?" inquired Dick.

"Fellow that rigged you. He's an uppish chap, but he's a leader with the upper classmen. Don't let him worry you."

This was a longer speech than Will usually made.

"But why should he be down on me because I've got money?" asked Dick. "It isn't my fault."

"Very exclusive school, this," explained Will. "Patronized by old, blue-blooded families, who pretend to have a horror of the newly-rich."

"But my father has been wealthy many years."

Will shrugged his shoulders.

"They seem to have a prejudice against you," he went on. "Don't mind. It'll wear off. Dutton—Ray Dutton's put 'em up to it. He's a cad. Don't mind him," and with that Will turned and walked away.

"Well, I guess I can get along without Dutton and his crowd," thought Dick. "Queer, I never supposed money would make this sort of a difference. It didn't at home. Well, I'll try to get along, but it's evidently going to be up-hill work. Still, I'll do it, and, if money stands in the way—well——"

Dick shrugged his shoulders in a sort of helpless fashion, and rejoined Paul. The two strolled about, noting the scenes taking place on every hand. They saw many cadets, obviously freshmen, and some of the latter introduced themselves to Dick and his companion. They were Franklin Boardman, Stanley Booker, Lyndon Butler and Eugene Graham.

"Let's stick together for a while," proposed 'Gene, as the boys called him. "It'll soon be grub time, I understand, and we'll sit near each other."

This suited the others, and, when the gong rang, summoning them to the mess hall, the six lads went in a body, finding seats in a row on one side of the long tables, which were served by colored waiters.

Discipline had not yet been put into force, and no one was in uniform. The mess hall was a lively place, for the older cadets were continually calling jokes back and forth to their chums, or jollying the waiters whom they knew of old.

Dick and his new acquaintances conversed together, and, in spite of their rather awkward feelings, managed to partake of a good meal, for Kentfield Academy was noted for the excellence of its cuisine.

When the meal was nearly over Toots appeared in the hall, with a hammer, and a piece of paper. He tacked a notice up on the bulletin board.

"Hey, Toots; what's that?" called Ray Dutton.

"Notice about appearing in uniform, Mr. Dutton," replied the odd soldier.

"When's it to be?"

"To-morrow morning."

"Aw, tear that down, Toots, you imitation brigadier general you!" called another youth.

"Sure. We don't want to tog up until the first of the week," added another. "Swallow that, Toots, and tell the commandant you lost it."

"Orders is orders," said Toots firmly, hammering in the last tack, and leaving the hall.

The afternoon was spent in assigning the new cadets to their classes, and arranging for the courses of study. They were told that formal drills would not begin until Monday, this being Thursday, nor would any recitations be heard until then.

After supper, or dinner as it was called at the academy, the new boys strolled about in little groups, Dick and his five friends keeping together.

"I wonder where all the older cadets are?" said Dick, as he looked about, and noticed that none was in sight.

"That's so, they have disappeared," added Lyndon Butler. "I wonder what that means?"

They did not have long to wait for an answer. A figure slid up to Dick, and, almost without turning he knew it to be Will. The silent youth spoke but one word:

"Hazing!"

Then he walked away as silently as he had approached, and Dick turned to his companions.

"I guess they're getting ready to haze us freshmen," he remarked.

"I thought they didn't haze here," said 'Gene Graham quickly. He was rather a small chap, and seemed very nervous.

"I guess they do it in spite of the rules," said Dick. "Well, the best way is to take what's coming, and bear it as well as you can. If you don't it will be unpleasant for you. I don't believe it will be very bad."

"Are you going to let 'em haze you?" asked Paul Drew.

"Sure," answered Dick.

"Then I guess I will, too."

"Well, I s'pose it's got to be," said little 'Gene with a sigh. "I hope they don't toss us in a blanket, though."

"If they do, just lie still, and you'll come down easy," advised Dick. "It'll soon be over."

That night, in their room, Dick and Paul heard the sound of footsteps along the corridor. Then came smothered cries, and strange sounds in the apartments adjoining.

"They're coming," whispered Paul.

Dick nodded grimly.

A moment later there came a soft knock on their portal.

"Well?" asked Dick, though he knew who it was.

"Open, in the name of the Ancient and Honorable Order of the Mystic Pig," came the demand in a whisper.

Dick opened the door, and in rushed several of the older cadets, led by Ray Dutton.

"Oh, we've drawn a millionaire!" Dutton cried, in sneering tones. "Well, take the other chap first, fellows. Lively, now, we've got a heap of 'em to initiate!"

Several lads seized Paul, who submitted with as good grace as possible.

CHAPTER VII

DICK THINKS HE HAS A CLUE

"What's it to be, Ray, the blanket, outside, or the ordeal of the pitcher?" asked one of the cadets holding Paul.

"The pitcher, I guess," answered Dutton. "The blanket's getting too tame, and we have so many to look after that we can't take 'em outside. Any water in the jug, Beeby?"

"Full," replied a fat lad, taking up one of the two pitchers in the room.

"Up with him!" commanded Dutton, and several cadets seized Paul in an instant. Before he knew what was happening they had stood him on his head, two of them holding each of his rather long legs upright.

"Hold open his trouser legs," said Dutton. "I'll do the pouring."

He had the pitcher full of water, and, as his fellow hazers made a sort of funnel of the two legs of the victim's trousers, Ray poured the contents of the water pitcher down them. The fluid spurted out at the unlucky new student's waist and collar, and ran in a little stream over the floor. Paul struggled but could not escape.

"Sop that up, fellows!" cried Dutton. "We don't want it to ruin the ceilings below. Use the bed clothes."

The other cadets, who were not holding Paul, grabbed the sheets and spreads from the neatly made beds, and piled them in the little pond of water on the floor.

"Hand me the other pitcher, Naylor," commanded the leader.

"Better save it for——" and Naylor glanced at Dick, who was standing quietly in a corner, under guard of several cadets, awaiting his turn.

"We'll not need it for him," replied Dutton. "Give it here."

Some one handed him the other pitcher full of water, and the fluid in that, a moment later, went gurgling down the inside of Paul's clothes, spurting out as had the other.

"You're initiated into the Ancient and Honorable Order of the Mystic Pig," announced Dutton, making a sign to his comrades to let Paul regain his feet. "Do you solemnly promise to be most respectful to your superiors, and not to partake of ham and eggs or any form of pork until after Christmas?"

"You'd better promise," said one of the cadets to Paul, who hesitated.

"Oh, I promise all right," he said, with a rueful smile as he looked down at his soaked garments, and surveyed the confusion in the room. There was not a dry article of bed clothing left.

"Now for the other one!" cried Beeby, making a grab for Dick.

The young millionaire was ready to submit to any form of hazing that might be inflicted, but, to his surprise Dutton said:

"Never mind him. We'll let him go."

"Why he's a freshman," objected several of the cadets, evidently thinking Dutton imagined Dick to be immune.

"I know it, but he's in a different class," went on the leader with a covert sneer. "He might buy up the police authorities and have us arrested for having a little fun. We'll let him alone. We're only after common mortals."

Dick flushed.

"You're mistaken," he said as calmly as he could. "If hazing is in order I'm ready to take my share. I assure you I won't squeal. I'm not that kind."

It hurt him, to think that he should be taken for a "squealer." He, Dick Hamilton, who had done his own share of hazing in the academy at home.

"No, thank you. It's too risky monkeying with millionaires," said Dutton. "Come on, fellows."

The band of hazing cadets filed out of Dick's room, bent on subjecting other students to their harmless pranks. As they left, Dick heard one of them say:

"Aw, Dutton, why didn't we try the rope and window game on him? It would have been sport. He looks like an all-right sort."

"He isn't in our class," replied the leader of the hazers. "He thinks his money can get him anything he wants, but he'll find out he's mistaken. It's a shame the faculty allowed him to come here, where only the best families are represented."

Dick heard it all plainly. He realized how he had been misjudged, but he resolved to live down the wrong opinion the other students seemed to have formed of him. Or perhaps they merely followed Dutton's leadership.

And so Dick was not hazed, though he was the only freshman in all the academy who escaped the ordeal, and, though many lads would gladly have dispensed with the ceremony, Dick Hamilton felt as if he would have parted with some of his fortune to have been included in the unfortunate class. For, had he been, it would have meant that he was considered as a future chum and comrade of the upperclassmen. But he had been left severely alone.

"Well, you got off lucky," commented Paul, as he began to remove his wet garments.

"Do you think so?" asked Dick, somewhat bitterly. "I rather wish they had given me what you got."

"Why?" asked his roommate.

Dick told his reasons.

"I don't see why they hold my money against me," he added.

"I heard some talk about it," admitted Paul. "Some of the older cadets have read the things printed in the papers about you; when you went out west to investigate that gold mine, and when you hired the circus to come to Hamilton Corners. They evidently think you depend on your money to win popularity, and I heard some of them say you were to be taught a lesson."

"They're beginning already," said Dick. "Perhaps you would rather not room with such an unpopular chap as I seem to be. I guess I could get an apartment alone, by paying double rates," he added, sarcastically.

"Nonsense!" exclaimed Paul. "I'm not that sort, and I don't believe you'll find many cadets who are. I don't care for money, one way or the other. I wish my dad had a little more. Don't let Dutton and his cronies worry you. You'll have friends among the freshmen, anyway."

"Not if Dutton has his say."

"Well, perhaps he won't have it. He comes of a very old family, I'm told, who have not much money, but who are very proud. I don't care for him myself, but he's considered a leader here."

"My, you certainly got a soaking," commented Dick, as Paul stripped. He was glad to change the unpleasant subject.

"I sure did," admitted the other "and what's more we've got to sleep in a damp bed, unless we ask the housekeeper for other covers."

"No, don't do that. I would give the hazing away, and I might become more unpopular than I am," and Dick laughed a little uneasily.

"I don't fancy sleeping between damp sheets, though."

"I've got an extra suit of pajamas in my case," said Dick. "You can put them on, and we'll stretch out on the beds without covers.

"It's not cold. We'll take our medicine. Or, rather, I'll share part of yours."

They passed a rather uncomfortable night, but did not think of complaining. In the morning they compared notes with the other freshmen, many of whom had had the same experience.

That day was spent in forming the new cadets into companies, and, to Dick's disgust he found that he was in the company of which Ray Dutton was the cadet captain, and John Stiver, a crony of the captain, was lieutenant. Paul Drew was in Company B, Dick's being designated as Company A. But our hero took some consolation from the fact that his odd friend William the Silent was a sergeant in his company.

The new cadets were given their rifles, made to don uniforms, put through a preliminary drill that afternoon, and told something of the routine that would be in order when matters had settled down into their usual grooves. Dick picked out his line of studies, received his text books and took them to his room, where he found Paul.

The next day being Saturday the cadets had the afternoon free and they strolled about the grounds, went off on horseback or rowing, as they desired. Somewhat to his regret Dick noticed that a rule was posted forbidding freshmen to go out rowing or riding alone after Saturday. They must be accompanied by a teacher or cadet officer.

"They must think we're babies," he murmured.

"Well, when we get to know the ropes a little better," said Paul, "we'll go out together."

That evening, when the mail was distributed, Dick received a letter from his father, posted just as the ship was sailing. There were also several missives from his chums at home, and quite a bulky letter, which when the young millionaire opened it, he saw was from aged Captain Handlee, and contained a photograph.

With many words, and a somewhat lengthy explanation, the old soldier stated that he had had copies made of the photograph of his son, and was sending one to Dick, to aid him in tracing the missing man.

"There, I nearly forgot about my promise," said Dick, recalling it as he saw the picture. "I must make some inquiries of Major Webster as soon as possible."

He took the photograph to his room, and placed it on a shelf, where he would be sure to see it, to remind him of his quest, though he had little hopes that it would amount to anything.

It was Sunday morning when Dick, who had awakened rather early, heard steps coming along the corridor, and then came the whistled strains of "Just Before the Battle, Mother," followed by the reveille, cheerily warbled.

"That's Toots," said Dick to Paul, who awakened just then.

Toots stopped outside Dick's door and knocked.

"Come," cried the young millionaire, and Toots, the odd character, entered, carrying a pail of hot water.

"One of the janitors is sick," he explained, "and I'm helping out. You can use this for shaving or drink it, just as you like," he added with a smile.

He filled the boys' hot water pitchers, and was about to leave the room, when he caught sight of the photograph of Corporal Bill Handlee on the shelf.

"Where—where did you get that?" he asked, turning quickly to the two lads.

"Why?" asked Dick, much impressed by the manner of Toots.

"Because I—I think I know him—or did once," and the man set down his pail of water, and drew his hand across his forehead, as if trying to brush away some cobwebs. Dick noticed that there was a scar on the man's brow.

"Where did you see him? When was it? Where was it?" asked Dick rapidly, thinking he had stumbled on a clue.

"I don't know—I can't recollect, but the face—that face seems familiar," and Toots, taking up the photo, gazed earnestly at it.

"That is the picture of the missing son of an old soldier who lives in Hamilton Corners," said Dick. "Captain Handlee asked me to make some inquiries about him. It's queer you should think you recognized it, Toots. Were you ever in the army?"

The man shook his head slowly.

"I don't know," he said. "I'm a fine shot though. I ought to be in the army."

Dick felt a new hope. The missing man said he was an expert marksman. But then Dick recalled what he had heard about Toots; that the man had a delusion that he was a sharpshooter, but that he could scarcely hit the outer edge of a big target.

"Can't you recall where you have seen this man?" asked Dick earnestly.

Toots slowly shook his head.

"What was his name?" he asked.

"Corporal Bill Handlee."

"No, that name doesn't sound familiar. But I'm sure I've seen him somewhere. I can't think—something seems to stop me here," and the man again passed his hand across his forehead.

"Try," urged Dick.

Toots made a strong effort to recall the past, but it was of no avail.

He shook his head once more, picked up his pail, and started out.

"I guess I'm mistaken," he said. "But some day you boys must come and see me shoot. I'm a dandy at it."

Then he went down the corridor whistling "The Star Spangled Banner," and ending up with a spirited rendition of the bugle call to charge.

"That's queer," murmured Dick. "I thought I was going to get some news for Captain Handlee. Well, I must inquire of Major Webster."

"Hark," exclaimed Paul, as a bugle sounded clear and crisp on the morning air.

"Reveille—first call! Ten minutes to dress and turn out," said Dick, who had been studying the rules, and he began to get into his uniform.

CHAPTER VIII

DICK GETS A FALL

At the chapel service, which the cadets were required to attend, Dick saw, for the first time, all his fellow students gathered together under one roof. They were a fine body of young men, and he felt proud that he was one of them. Every one was in full dress uniform, and a spick and span appearance the lads made, as they marched to and from chapel, to the music of the cadet band.

Sunday seemed quite long to Dick, but he managed to spend some pleasant hours, strolling about with Paul Drew, and some other new cadets. He was glad, however, when Monday came, bringing with it many duties.

For the next two weeks Dick was kept so busy, being initiated into the mysteries of the drill, guard mounting, parade, marching in different formations, learning the meaning of the military commands, his studies and preparing for inspection, that he had little time to think of other matters.

He found opportunity to ask Major Webster concerning missing Bill Handlee, and the tactical officer made some inquiries of the war office, but all to no effect. All trace of the veteran's son seemed to have vanished.

"But what do you suppose made Toots—I mean Sam Sander—think he recognized the photo?" asked Dick.

"Well, you know poor Sam isn't quite right in his head," replied the major kindly. "He received an injury some years ago, I understand. You can see the scar on his forehead now. That made him rather simple minded, though he is a good worker, and very useful."

"Then I'm afraid I can't send Captain Handlee any good news."

"I'm afraid not, Hamilton."

Dick had to write the sorrowful tidings to the old soldier, much to his regret. The young millionaire also sent a missive to his father, telling something of the life at the academy, but saying nothing of the manner in which he had been treated. Dick bravely resolved to fight his own battles.

He found the studies anything but easy, but as he applied himself to his books, he stood well in his class.

In the meantime matters were beginning to move with military regularity, and the cadets in their natty uniforms, presented at drill, or inspection, inspiring pictures.

At first Dick, and all the new cadets, were rather awkward at drill, but this was to be expected, and little was thought of it. On several occasions though, Captain Dutton, who was in command over Dick, made sneering remarks evidently intended for our hero, who, however, did not reply.

With the exception of Sunday and Monday, the same general routine was followed. Reveille was sounded at six o'clock, with a second call ten minutes later. Then came "police" inspection, and woe betide the youth who was not spick and span. Sick call followed, but usually it was a mere form, for the cadets were as healthy as Spartans.

On Monday there was always general inspection, when it behooved Dick and his fellows to have their quarters in good order. Plenty of time was allowed for study and recitation, and there was much attention given to military life. There were lectures on tactics, and they were followed by practical illustrations.

"I wish they'd let us have a chance at the horses," remarked Dick, to Paul, when they were studying in their room one evening. "The older cadets have plenty of cavalry drill, but we have to march around, carrying heavy guns, and doing all sorts of stunts like that."

"I understand we're to have our innings next week."

"Is that so? Good!"

Dick, and many other of the new cadets who loved horses were pleased to see a notice posted, a few days after this, stating that instructions in riding, and cavalry exercises, were to be given in the big shed and would begin the following Monday.

"Now we'll have some fun," said Dick. "Aren't you glad, Paul?"

"Well, I don't care much about horses. I feel safer on my feet."

"Oh, you'll get used to a horse soon enough, and then you'll never want to walk."

There were good horses in the academy stables, and, to his delight, a fine mount was assigned to Dick. He made friends with the animal at once, and when the "awkward squad" was put through their paces, Dick earned commendation from the drill master for the excellent seat he maintained.

For a week or more Dick and his fellow freshmen practiced every day in the riding hall. The cadets who at first sat insecurely in the saddle were beginning to learn how to maintain themselves, and one afternoon the drill master announced that the next day they would be allowed to go out on the cavalry plain.

"That's the stuff!" cried Dick. "I've been wanting a good gallop for a long time."

"Guess we won't have much chance to gallop," replied Paul, who had been transferred to Dick's company. "Dutton's so mean he'll probably keep us at an easy walk. He thinks no one knows how to ride but him."

"I'll show him, if I get a chance," murmured Dick.

The cadets were formed into four companies the next day, and sent out on the cavalry plain for practice.

"Now I don't want any exhibitions of fancy riding," announced Ray Dutton, as he led the cadets over whom he had charge out from the drill hall. "You've got to creep before you walk, you know. Just take it easy, and we'll make a few circuits of the grounds."

"Pity he wouldn't let us gallop," said Dick, in a low voice to Paul, beside whom he was riding.

"Silence in the ranks!" exclaimed the cadet captain sharply. "Hamilton, if you speak again I'll report you."

Dick felt the hot blood mount to his face, but he kept his temper.

They went around at a slow pace, many of the lads chaffing under the restraint. Then Dutton gave the command to trot, and they let their horses out a trifle.

Whether something frightened Dick's horse, or whether the animal wanted to take a good run and show the others what he could do, it was impossible to say. At any rate our hero's steed gave a sudden spring, and, rushing through the opened ranks of the cadet horsemen ahead of him, sailed past Captain Dutton at a fast gait.

"Halt!" cried the leading cadet. "Where are you going, Hamilton? Come back here at once! I'll report you! Come back!"

Dick tried to rein his horse in, but the animal had the bit in his teeth, and it was useless to pull on the leather. Still the young millionaire was not frightened. He knew he could manage the animal.

But Dutton, with a muttered exclamation, spurred after Dick.

"Halt!" he cried again. "Halt, or I'll place you under arrest for disobeying orders!"

"I can't stop him!" Dick flung back, over his shoulder.

Dutton's horse was a fast one, and he soon caught up to the young cadet. He crossed in front of him, wheeled about and, a moment later the two horses collided violently. Dick was flung up in the air, and, the next instant, came heavily to the ground, where he lay quiet, while his horse bolted.

Dutton, who had retained his seat, looked down on the prostrate figure.

"Come. Get up," he said. "No shamming."

Dick did not move.

"Here, Drew, Butler, Graham!" called Captain Dutton. "Here's a chance to practice first aid to the injured. See what's the matter with him."

The three cadets he had named galloped forward, while the remainder of the company came to a halt.

CHAPTER IX

WHO FIRED THE GUN?

"Pick him up, and see if he's hurt," ordered Dutton though he did not take the trouble to get off his horse to ascertain. "Very likely he's only shamming."

But is needed only a look at Dick's pale face to show that he had had a hard fall. The breath was knocked out of him.

The three cadets bent over him, and, while one raised him to a sitting position, the others chaffed his hands. Dick opened his eyes, and stared wonderingly about him.

"What—what—where am I?" he asked, and then he saw the mounted students, he added, "I fell."

"Are you hurt?" asked Graham.

"No—no, I guess not."

But when Dick tried to stand he found he was so dizzy that his fellow cadets had to support him.

"Take him back to the hospital," ordered Dutton, "and then you three rejoin your company."

At that moment Major Webster, who had been drilling some of the older cadets, in advanced tactics on a distant part of the field, came galloping up.

"What has happened?" he asked. "Ah, Hamilton, eh? Are you hurt?"

"I fell off my horse. He bolted with me," replied Dick.

"Are you sure you're not hurt?"

"Yes; only a trifle dizzy."

"I'm sending him back to the hospital," announced Dutton.

"That's proper. Are you sure you'll be all right, Hamilton?" asked the major kindly.

"Oh, yes. I believe I can ride now."

"No, I can't allow it. You must take a rest."

On the way back with the cadets, Dick insisted that he could go alone, and did not need help.

"Orders are orders," replied Graham with a smile. "Dutton might make a fuss if we didn't do as he said."

"It was all his fault," added Paul Drew. "He deliberately collided with you, Dick."

"Oh, no; I hardly think he would do that!"

"But he did," insisted Butler. "He didn't need to gallop in front of you that way. I looked just as if he wanted to unseat you, didn't it, fellows?"

"That's right," added Paul. "I'd report him if I were you."

"Oh, no," answered Dick quickly. "There's no use making trouble. Even if he did do it on purpose, I wouldn't gain anything by reporting him. I'm no squealer."

"But you might have been badly hurt," said Butler.

"I wasn't though, and a miss is as good as a mile."

"That's a good way of looking at it," commented Paul. "I'd feel like fighting him, if he did that to me."

"Say, I'm all right. There's no need for you fellows to come back with me," went on Dick.

"If we don't Dutton may make a row," objected Butler. "We'd better do it."

Not wanting to get his fellow cadets into trouble, Dick allowed them to accompany him to the hospital, which was maintained by the academy. There the surgeon in charge, a grizzled war veteran, felt of our hero's bones, and announced, gruffly, that he was all right, but that he had better rest a while.

Which Dick was glad enough to do, as his head was beginning to ache.

"Dutton must want to get rid of me," he thought, as he stretched out on the bed in his room. "If he keeps on I shall certainly have a clash with him, and then I s'pose there'll be trouble. I don't want to fight, but I'm not going to submit to his meanness. I certainly am under a handicap here. I wish I could ask dad to send me to some other school. No, I don't either. I'll fight it out here, and I'll win, too, or I'll know the reason why!"

Major Webster, when he returned from the drill, inquired how Dick felt, and received the assurance that the lad was all right.

"We must give you a quieter horse," he said with a smile.

"Oh, no, I can manage him all right," said Dick. "Captain Dutton—er—he and I happened to collide, or it never would have happened."

"Strange, Dutton is an excellent rider," commented the major as he walked away.

A slight headache the next day was all the ill effect that Dick experienced from his tumble. He appeared at chapel, and took part in all the day's duties. For a week or more life went on rather uneventfully at the academy. Dick had a letter from his father, stating that business was likely to keep him abroad longer than he expected.

Dick also got a letter from Henry Darby, giving some news of Hamilton Corners, and telling how Dick's chums missed him. The letter closed with this:

"Grit misses you very much. He doesn't eat hardly anything, and he lies in his kennel all day."

"Poor Grit," said Dick to Paul, and he told of his bulldog. "I wish I could have him here with me."

"Why don't you?" suggested his roommate. "Some of the other cadets are allowed special privileges, why don't you ask if you can bring Grit here? You could keep him in the stable."

"I believe I will," said Dick, and he sought and received permission from Colonel Masterly to do this.

A few days later Grit arrived, and he was probably the happiest dog living, as Dick took him out of the shipping crate. The animal bounded about, and fairly leaped over his master's head in the excess of his joy.

Grit made friends with such few chums as Dick had among the freshmen, and they were not many, for Dutton's influence seemed even to extend to them. The advent of the bulldog appeared to further arouse the ire of the young captain.

"I expect our millionaire cadet will be having a private menagerie next," he said with a sneer. "But I tell you one thing, Hamilton, if I catch the brute around my quarters I'll kick him out."

"I shouldn't advise you to try it," said Dick coolly. "It might not be healthy—for you."

"Do you mean that you'd attack me?" asked Dutton, taking a step toward Dick.

"No, but Grit might; eh, Grit, old boy."

The dog growled in a menacing manner, and Dutton, turning on his heel, made off up the campus, but the scowl he gave Dick augured anything but well for the young millionaire.

It was about a week after this when, one evening, Dick, who was sitting in his room, studying with Paul, suddenly exclaimed:

"There, I've left my algebra out under the three elms. I was studying there this afternoon."

The three elms were a clump of giant trees on the campus, and a recognized stamping ground for the freshmen, who frequently studied there, when it was too hot in their rooms.

"Better go out and get it," advised Paul. "It looks like rain, and you know it means a demerit to have soiled books."

"Guess I'll slip out and get it," decided Dick. "I'll have just about time enough before taps."

He started down the long corridor, but he had not taken a dozen steps before taps was sounded on the bugle, the plaintive call of "lights out" vibrating clearly on the night air.

"Better come back," advised Paul, from the open door of their room, as he prepared to turn out the electric lamp.

"No, I think I'll chance it," decided Dick. "No one is likely to see me, and I might as well get a demerit for this as for having a rain-soaked algebra. Leave the door open so I can find the place in the dark."

He kept on, stealing quietly down the hall. Paul went to bed, and was just dozing off when he was startled by the loud report of the cannon used for firing the sunrise and sunset guns. The echoes thundered among the academy buildings, and were re-echoed from the distant hills. Paul arose. Clearly some of the cadets were up to a trick, and had fired the gun.

A few minutes later Dick came running into the room.

"Did you get the book? Who fired the gun?" asked Paul in a whisper.

"Yes, I got the algebra, and, just as I did the gun went off. I saw some of the fellows running, and of course I was running too, but, just as I was coming in, Stiver, who is doing guard duty, saw me."

"What did he say?"

"Called to me halt, but I didn't."

"He'll report you, and you may be blamed for—"

An instant later the tramp of feet was heard in the corridor.

"It's inspection!" gasped Paul. "Undress quick, and get into bed!"

CHAPTER X

DICK HAS A FIGHT

But it was too late. The door of Dick's room was pushed open, and, in the light of the incandescent that burned in the hall, the two cadets could see Captain Hayden and several of the instructors looking in.

"Hamilton—Drew—are you here?" asked Captain Hayden sharply.

"Yes, sir," replied Dick, but an instant later the light revealed him fully dressed, whereas he should have been in bed at taps.

"Ha!" exclaimed the head master. "This will bear investigation. Why aren't you in bed, Hamilton?"

"I went down to get my algebra, which I left under the elms."

"Did you have anything to do with firing the saluting gun?"

"No, sir."

"I will have to investigate. Report in my room in ten minutes."

Captain Hayden marched on, and the two cadets could hear distant sounds that indicated a general inspection of quarters.

"I guess you're in for it, Dick," said Paul.

"I can prove what I went out for."

"Maybe. But I wonder who fired that gun?"

"I don't know. Some of the older cadets likely. Well, I s'pose I've got to go to Captain Hayden's room."

Dick found several other students gathered in the reception apartment of the head master. They were lads who had been found still up when their rooms were hurriedly entered after the blowing of taps, and the firing of the gun.

"Who was captain of the guard?" asked Captain Hayden, when he came in and faced a rather frightened lot of cadets.

"I was, sir," replied John Stiver.

"What did you see?"

"I was on duty, sir, near the main entrance of the south barracks, and the first I knew I saw the flash of the gun, and heard it go off."

"What else did you see?"

"I saw a cadet run from the campus into the barracks. He would not halt when I called to him."

"Who was it?"

"I don't like to say, sir."

"Very likely not, but you must."

"It was—it was Hamilton, sir."

"Ha!" exclaimed the head master.

"I went to the three elms to get my algebra which I had forgotten," said Dick.

"After taps?"

"Yes, sir."

"Then you broke one of the rules."

"Yes, sir, but I thought that if it rained, and my book got wet, I'd get a demerit for that, so I decided I would take a chance on going after taps. I started before the bugle sounded."

"Ha! I will look into that afterward. You are sure you were not near the gun?"

"Yes, sir."

"I might add," went on Stiver, "that, after I called to Hamilton to halt, and he would not, I saw his dog running after him, and the animal seemed to have something tied to its tail."

"To it's tail?"

"Yes, sir."

"What was it?"

"It seemed like a piece of string."

"A piece of string. That may explain it. Hamilton, what do you know of this?"

"Nothing, Captain Hayden. Grit was not with me. I left him in his kennel, in the stable, chained up."

"We must look into this. Lieutenant Stiver, tell Sander to bring the bulldog here."

"Perhaps I had better go along," suggested Dick. "Grit might make a fuss."

"If he goes, you had better make sure he doesn't slip the string off the dog's tail," put in Dutton, with a sneer.

Dick started, and looked angrily at his enemy.

"That will do, Dutton," said Captain Hayden quietly. "You may accompany Sander, Hamilton."

Toots, who was on hand, started for the stables, followed by Dick.

"Are you going to get into trouble?" asked the old man, who had taken quite a fancy to our hero.

"I hope not. If Grit had anything to do with firing the gun, by means of a string tied to his tail, some one who had a grudge against me is responsible for it."

"I'm sure of it, Mr. Hamilton," and Toots marched on, whistling "Dixy Land," ending up with a series of bugle calls.

They found Grit cowering in his kennel, as if much frightened. Dick and Toots looked him over. Sure enough there was a stout piece of cord tied to his stump of a tail.

"It looks bad," commented Toots.

"I'm not worried," declared Dick.

Captain Hayden looked grave, when Toots handed him the bit of cord. He sent Sander to the saluting gun, and Toots returned presently with same cord, which matched that taken from Grit's tail.

"Was this on the gun?" asked the head master.

"Attached to a primer, that had been fired," replied Toots.

"Hamilton," began Captain Hayden, "I don't like to accuse you on such circumstantial evidence, but it looks—"

"I had nothing to do with firing the gun," said Dick quickly. "If my dog did it, some one else tied the string to his tail."

"Whom do you suspect?"

"I don't know."

"If you please, sir," spoke up Graham, "I don't think Hamilton had anything to do with firing the gun."

"Why not?"

"Because my window is right opposite it. I was looking out, just before it went off, and I saw a crowd of students near it. They had a dog, for I could hear him growl, and I heard some one say 'look out or the brute will put his teeth in you.' Then some one else said, 'I guess I can manage him.' If Hamilton had been there I don't believe Grit would have growled."

"He certainly would not," said Dick, noticing that Dutton was scowling at Graham.

"Ha! Hum," mused the head master. "I believe you are right, Graham. Hamilton, you are practically exonerated, but this matter will not be allowed to drop. Firing the gun was a serious infraction of the rules, and dangerous in the bargain. Whoever fired it must have stolen into the ammunition house, which is a risky thing to do, especially in the dark."

"I am glad you don't think I did it, sir," said Dick to Captain Hayden.

"I am glad, also, but I shall have to mark you five off for being out after taps. When I find out who fired the gun I shall punish them severely. It seems as though it was done to throw suspicion on you."

"That is what I think," said Dick quickly.

"Whom do you suspect?"

"I had rather not say, sir."

"Of course not, no, I wouldn't want you to on mere suspicion. You young gentlemen may retire to your rooms, now. I will look into this matter further."

The cadets filed out, all of them breathing easier. As Dutton passed Dick in the hall, he said:

"Did you refer to me when you said you suspected some one?"

"Not particularly."

"You looked at me," said the cadet captain angrily.

"Well, a cat may look at a king, I suppose."

"None of your impertinence."

"I'm not impertinent, but I don't propose to have you dictate to me."

"You'll have to, as long as you're a freshman. I say you intimated that I fired that gun and tried to throw the blame on you."

"I can't help what you say."

"Do you believe I did it?"

"I refuse to answer."

"Then I'll make you! Take that!" and before Dick could step back Dutton had hit him a blow in the face. "You know what that means, I suppose," said Dutton with a sneer.

"A fight?" asked Dick quietly.

"Of course. I'll send a friend to you to-morrow and we'll see if you'll back up your words."

"Don't worry. I'll be on hand," replied Dick, as he went to his room.

He told Paul of what had happened, and the latter consented to act as second to him in the fight. The matter was quietly arranged, and, the next afternoon Dick, and the few chums he had, slipped off after the evening parade to a secluded spot, where all the fistic battles of the academy took place. Dutton and a large throng of his supporters were on hand, and the preliminaries were soon settled.

"Time!" called Lieutenant Stiver, who acted as Dutton's second.

The two youths faced each other, but dispensed with the ceremony of shaking hands. The next moment Dutton aimed a blow at Dick's face, but our hero cleverly dodged and sent a stiff right hander to the cadet captain's jaw.

CHAPTER XI

DICK GIVES A SPREAD

The shock of the blow made Dutton stagger back, but he quickly regained his balance, and rushed at Dick, raising his foot to give him a kick.

"Hold on, that's not fair!" cried Paul. "Do you stand for that, Stiver?"

Stiver plainly wanted to side with Dutton, but there were cries of "Shame! That's not fair!" from several in the crowd and Dutton's second was forced to caution his man.

"Don't do that, Dutton," he said. "You can lick him with your fists."

"Yes, and I'll fix him, all right!" exclaimed the angry cadet captain.

Dick, who had stepped back, out of reach of his opponent's foot, now stood up to meet the rush of Dutton.

"There! I guess that will teach you to make insinuations about me!" spluttered the angry lad, as he aimed a fierce blow at Dick. Our hero easily dodged it, however, and countered with a stiff upper cut, which gave Dutton quite a jolt.

Dick was not quite quick enough in getting away, however, and received a blow on the chest, which he did not mind, much. Then Dutton closed in, and both boys exchanged several severe blows, but Dick had the best of it, for he had taken boxing lessons from an experienced instructor at home.

"Go in and do him!" called Dutton's friends.

"Stand up to him, Dick," advised Paul, in low tones at the conclusion of the first round. "You've got him going."

Dutton tried to be calm as he came up the second time, but he speedily lost his temper, as he saw how easily Dick parried his blows.

"Why don't you stand up and fight?" he asked.

"Why don't you hit me?" retorted Dick, as he tapped his antagonist on the nose, making it bleed slightly.

"I'll pay you for that!" cried Dutton, rushing forward.

"Not so loud!" cautioned Stiver. "You'll bring some of the professors down on us."

Once more Dick dodged a straight left hander, and, in return, sent in a terrific right, that caught Dutton on the point of the jaw. The cadet went down like a log, and lay still.

"You've knocked him out, Hamilton," remarked one of the older cadets, who acted as referee. "I congratulate you."

"Yes, he fought well," added another, but there was no heartiness in his tones, and, to Dick, it seemed almost as if they were sorry he had won.

For won he had, as Dutton did not arise. He had been fairly, but harmlessly, knocked out.

"Do you throw up the sponge?" asked Paul, of Stiver.

"I guess so," was the rather surly response. "Your man wins."

"I hope I didn't hurt him," said Dick. "I didn't mean to hit so hard, but he rushed right into it."

"You didn't hurt me!" suddenly exclaimed Dutton, as he struggled to his feet. "I'm game yet."

"You've had enough," said his second. "You can have another try later."

"I can do him," mumbled Dutton, but even his friends were forced to admit that he had been well beaten.

"Will you shake hands?" asked Dick, advancing toward his antagonist.

"No!" exclaimed Dutton, surlily.

A hot flush came to Dick's face, and he was about to turn away when, the older cadet, who had complimented him said:

"Shake hands, Dutton. Don't be a cad."

This was equivalent to a command, and Dutton grudingly complied.

"Do you think he will be better friends with you after this?" asked Paul, as he and Dick walked away together.

"I hope so, but I doubt it."

Dick was right. Though he had gained the victory he had whipped one of the most popular cadets, which Dutton was, in spite of his caddishness.

Our hero's victory took nothing away from the regard in which Dutton was held, while, as for Dick, save a few friends whom he had made among the younger lads, he was not admitted to the comradeship of the older cadets, to which place, of right, he belonged. The fight had not made him popular, as he had hoped it would, after he had won it, though the sporting element in the academy could not but admire his fistic abilities.

"I don't seem to be making much progress," remarked Dick to his roommate, one afternoon. "You have more friends than I have."

"Oh, I don't think so."

"Yes, you have. It would be different, if I was at home, but here, everyone seems to follow Dutton's lead, and turns a cold shoulder to me."

"Maybe you'll have more acquaintances next term."

"I doubt it. I wish I could get in with the fellows. They'll be making up the football eleven, soon, and I'd like a chance to play."

"Do you play?"

"I did at home. I was right half-back. But I don't s'pose I'll have any show here."

"I tell you what you might do," said Paul, after a pause. "Why don't you give a spread?"

"A spread?"

"Yes, a feast, you know. You can get permission to have it in one of the rooms, and you can invite a lot of the fellows. Several of the new fellows have done that, and some of them got proposed for membership in the Sacred Pig society."

This was one of the exclusive secret organizations of the academy, and Dick, as well as many others, wished to join. But one had to be invited to apply for membership, and only those students on whom the seal of approval was set by the older cadets had this honor.

"Do you think that would do any good?" asked Dick.

"It might."

"Then I'll try. Here's a chance where I can use some of my money. If this plan doesn't work, I have another that I'll spring."

"What is it?"

"Well, I don't want to say yet. I may want to get you to help me at it, though."

"I'll do anything I can."

"I know you will, Paul. I wish there were more like you."

Dick obtained permission from Colonel Masterly to give a spread in one of the barrack rooms, and he made elaborate preparations for it. A town caterer was given orders to supply a fine supper, and then Dick sent out his invitations. He included all the lads in his class, and every member of the so-called "sporting crowd."

"Are you going to invite Dutton?" asked Paul.

"Of course. I want him more than all the others. If he would drop his hard feelings we could be friends."

"After he tried to get you into trouble about your dog, and the firing of the cannon?"

"Do you think he did?"

"I'm sure of it, and so are lots of others."

"Captain Hayden can't seem to find out anything about it."

"No, because all of Dutton's cronies are keeping mum. But I'm sure he did it."

"Well, I'll forgive him, if he'll be friends. I got even by whipping him, I guess."

"Perhaps, though I don't believe he thinks so."

Dick received acceptances from nearly all the lads in his class, but regarding the others he heard nothing, and did not know whether they would come or not. He hoped they would—particularly Dutton and his chums.

On the afternoon of the evening on which Dick's spread was to come off, he met Dutton and Stiver on the campus.

"Let's see, isn't your spread to-morrow night?" asked Stiver, with studied carelessness.

"It's to-night," said Dick, pleasantly. "I hope you are both coming."

"I'll see," answered Stiver.

"Is there going to be anything to drink?" asked Dutton with a covert sneer.

"Lemonade," replied Dick promptly.

"Is that all? I should think a millionaire cadet like you would provide champagne; or at least beer."

"It's against the rules," said Dick.

"Then you'll have some cigars."

"No."

"Cigarettes then?"

"No."

"I suppose you'll give us malted milk and crackers," sneered Dutton, as he turned aside. "I don't think that will suit us. Eh, Stiver?"

"No indeed. I thought you wanted to be a sport, Hamilton?"

"I don't care about breaking rules," replied Dick. "Besides, I don't use tobacco or liquor."

"Ah, he's a regular Sunday school brand of millionaire," remarked Dutton, with a mean laugh. "He gives his money to the heathen, instead of buying cigars. Come on, Stiver."

At Dick's spread, that night, only a few freshmen came, and, though they tried to be jolly, the affair was a dismal failure, after the elaborate preparations that had been made. None of Dutton's friends came, and not a member of the sporting element.

"Dutton told 'em to stay away," said Paul, as he and Dick went to their room, after it was all over.

"I suppose so," answered Dick gloomily, and there was a heavy feeling in his heart, that the thought of all his wealth could not lighten.

He was beginning to realize what it meant to fulfill the conditions of his mother's will.

CHAPTER XII

AN ANGRY FARMER

"Say, Dick," remarked Paul, the next morning, as they leaped out of bed at the sound of the bugle giving the first call, "that spread must have cost you a pretty penny."

"I don't mind that a bit," replied the young millionaire, as he struggled into his uniform. "I'd be willing to spend a lot more if only the fellows would have come. But there's no use crying over spilled milk, as my dad says. Hurry up, Paul. Get this room in shape, or we'll be in for some bad marks at inspection."

The cadets quickly had their apartment in good order, and then got ready for breakfast.

They were a fine lot of cadets who filed into the mess hall a little later, well set-up young fellows, each with his uniform spick and span, marching with regular step that nearly approached the perfection of the trained soldier. For, such was the discipline at Kentfield, that even green lads quickly fell into the routine, and by this time Dick and the other freshmen carriedthemselves almost as well as did the senior students.

"Ah, that'll be some fun," remarked Paul, as they were leaving the mess-hall after the meal.

"What?" asked Dick.

"Target practice. There's a notice on the bulletin board that we're to have it right after the first study period. Are you a good shot?"

"I used to be, but the guns here are heavier than I'm accustomed to. I don't believe I can do as well."

"Oh, I guess you can. I hear that some of the third year lads can't do very extra."

There were two target ranges at Kentfield, one for long distance shooting, in the open, and the other in a rifle pit, indoors. It was there that a number of the cadets and their officers assembled a little later. Toots, who was a sort of janitor about the pits, was on hand.

"Ah, Toots, going to show us how to shoot to-day?" asked a student.

"Sure," replied Sam. "I'll give you a few lessons. Lend me your gun."

"Here you go, Tootsy old chap," added another cadet, passing over his rifle.

As all the cadets had not yet arrived discipline was rather lax, and the officers made no objection.

"Here's where I crack the bullseye first shot!" exclaimed Toots. He handled the gun as though he had long been used to it, and took quick aim. A sharp report followed, but there was no corresponding "ping" of the target to indicate a shot.

"Ha! Ha! Toots, you missed it altogether," cried Russell Glen, a first-year and somewhat sporty student in Dick's class.

"No, I didn't neither!" objected Sam. "It went clean through the target, that's why you didn't hear it. I'm a crack shot I am."

He really appeared to believe it, and was much disappointed when the marker called back that the bullet had gone about a foot over the target.

"Try again, Toots," said Glen.

"I will. This time I'll go right in the center."

Once more he fired, and the resulting laugh told that he had again missed.

"I guess this is your off day," observed Captain Dutton.

"Looks like it," remarked Toots ruefully, as he walked off, whistling "In a Prison Cell I Sit," and ending with the bugle call to charge.

The target practice soon began, and Dick, to his own surprise, made a good score, getting forty-nine out of a possible fifty.

"We have decided to have a practice march, around the lake, to-morrow," Major Webster announced to the cadets after target practice was over. "Fatigue uniforms of khaki will be worn, and the affair will last all day. Lunch will be taken in the field. You know the regulations, Captain Dutton, so inform your command of them, and be ready after reveille to-morrow."

The major paused, Captain Dutton saluted, and his superior officer turned away, his sword clanking at his heels.

"A practice march!" exclaimed Paul to Dick. "That will be sport."

"It sure will," added Dick.

"Silence in the ranks;" cried Dutton, in a dictatorial manner. "Lieutenant Stiver, watch Hamilton, I think he talks altogether too much."

It was an unjust accusation, but Dick knew better than to answer back.

That afternoon further instructions were issued regarding the practice march. The cadets would take one ration with them, and a wagon containing utensils for making coffee, etc., would accompany the amateur soldiers. They would have their rifles with them, and, during the day would have practice in skirmish firing, in throwing up trenches, and advancing on an imaginary enemy.

They started off soon after breakfast, led by Colonel Masterly, Major Rockford and Major Webster, while the cadet officers were in charge of the four companies, A, B, C and D.

It was a fine day in October, just right for a march, and the cadets presented a neat appearance, as, headed by the superior officers on horseback, they marched along the shores of the lake, off towards a wooded plain. The boys were attired in blue flannel shirts, khaki trousers and leggings.

"I hope they have more of these hikes before winter," remarked Paul to Dick.

"'Hike?' is that what you call 'em?"

"That's what the regulars do. It's a good name, I think."

"It sure is. Say, you get a fine view of the lake here."

The boys talked on, for there were no rules against it, and the experience of the march was a new one for many of them, including Dick.

They reached some suitable ground about ten o'clock and on orders from Major Webster the companies were formed into one command, under his direction. Then, an imaginary enemy having been located in a clump of woodland, the cadets were sent forward on the run, in skirmish parties, firing at will, and in volleys.

"Advance, and form trenches!" suddenly ordered the major.

The lads, using their bayonets as spades, and scooping the dirt up with their hands, soon formed shallow ditches, with an embankment of earth in front, and, lying prone behind this, ruthlessly mowed down the ranks of the enemy who still refused to show himself.

The rattle and bang of the rifles, the clouds of smoke, the flashes of fire, mingled with the hoarse commands of the major who was a war veteran; the rushing forward of the cadets, and their activity in digging trenches, made the scene one of excitement. It was glorious sport, Dick thought.

Tired, dusty and warm, though willing to keep at this war game indefinitely, the young soldiers finally reached the edge of the woods, where, having dislodged the enemy, they were conceded to have won a victory, and the march was again taken up.

A halt for dinner was made beside a little brook. Toots, who had charge of the provision wagon brought it up, and proceeded to build fires to make coffee.

"Toots, you old scoundrel," affectionately exclaimed a senior cadet, "did you bring the cream for my coffee?"

"Yes, Mr. Morton. I brought a jug full," replied Toots, who entered into the spirit of the fun.

"And I want a white table cloth," stipulated another.

"I've got one up my sleeve," answered Toots, busying himself about the wagon.

Campfires were soon ablaze, and the appetizing smell of coffee and steaks filled the air. The cadets opened their haversacks, and were preparing to eat, having formed into little informal groups, each company by itself.

"Say, Stiver," remarked Dutton, to his lieutenant, looking at a field of late sweet corn, which was near where they were camped, "I'd like a few of those ears to roast. How about you?"

"Sure's you're a foot high; but you know the orders. Mustn't do any foraging."

"Ah, what's the rule between friends? Besides, Colonel Masterly and Major Webster are away over on the other side of the woods. Send some of the freshmen after some corn."

"I'm not going to. You can if you want to."

"I will. Here, Boardman, you and Booker and Hamilton go and get some of that green corn."

"I'll not," replied Dick promptly, who knew that this refusal to obey his superior officer would be upheld, if, indeed, Dutton would dare prefer a charge against him.

"Afraid, eh?" sneered the young captain. "Very well, then, you take Hamilton's place, Butler."

The three lads designated, either being afraid to incur Dutton's displeasure, or because they wanted some of the corn, quietly sneaked into the field, and quickly returned with big armsful, which were soon put to roast, the husks being concealed under the leaves in the woods.

"Maybe, you'll have some?" asked Dutton, in sneering tones, of Dick, as the captain and his cronies began eating the roast corn.

"No thank you. Not that I don't like it, but I prefer to get it another way."

Dick felt that he was putting himself further than ever beyond the pale of his comrades' liking by his conduct, but he could not help it.

The lunch was almost over, and most of the corn had disappeared, when an elderly man, evidently a farmer, crawled through the fence near where Dick's company was. There was an angry look on his face.

"Which of you lads stole my corn?" he demanded. "And besides that you trampled down a lot. Who done it? That's what I want to know."

There was no need to answer. The evidences of the stolen corn were all about.

"I'm going to report this to Colonel Masterly," said the farmer, striding off toward where the superintendent was talking to the two majors.

CHAPTER XIII

A NARROW ESCAPE

"Hold on!" cried Dutton, springing to his feet. "Wait a minute, Mr.—er—Mr.—"

"No, you can't come any game like that over me!" cried the angry farmer. "You stole my corn, and trampled a lot of it down. That's agin orders, an' I know it. I'll report to your superior officers, and we'll see how you'll like it."

"But—er—but I say—" stammered Dutton, wishing he could do something to placate the man, for he knew that all the blame would fall on him, and that he would be severely dealt with; perhaps reduced to the ranks.

"No. I'll not listen to you," replied the farmer. "I'm going to report to Colonel Masterly."

"Now look at the mess you've got us into, Dutton," said Stiver. "Why couldn't you let the corn alone."

"Shut up!" retorted the cadet captain. "I say, Mr.—Mr. Farmer," he called after the man.

"My name's not Farmer, but I know what yours will be; it'll be Mud, soon. I'll teach you tin soldiers to spoil my corn."

There were murmurs among the cadets. They feared lest the whole company might be punished. But a scheme had come into Dick Hamilton's mind. Without asking permission from Dutton he hurried after the farmer.

"How much will pay for the damage to your corn, and what the boys took," he asked quietly, holding out a roll of bills, for Dick never was without a substantial sum.

"Now you're talking, sonny," said the farmer, a different look coming into his face. "Why didn't that captain of yours say so at first?"

"What's the damage?" asked Dick. From experience he had learned that cash will make up for almost any kind of a hurt.

"Wa'al, seein' as that was particularly fine corn, I'll have to charge you ten dollars for what ye took, and what damage ye done."

"Ten dollars! That's too much!" cried Paul Drew. "Don't pay it, Dick."

"Wa'al, then I'll see the colonel. I guess he'll pay that, rather than have his school sued," said the angry man.

"Here are ten dollars," said Dick quietly, handing over a bill. "I guess the boys found the corn worth it," he added with a smile.

"That's all right," said the farmer, as he pocketed the money. "I wouldn't 'a made a fuss if I'd a knowed you was goin' to pay for it. I'm reasonable, I am."

"Not at selling corn," murmured Paul, as the man went back into his field.

"Hurrah for Hamilton!" cried several cadets, who realized what Dick's action meant for them. "He's all right."

"He got us out of a bad scrape," observed Lieutenant Stiver. "My record won't stand many more demerits."

But instead of thanking Dick, Dutton turned aside. He acted as if he disliked to be under any obligations to the cadet who he so unreasonably hated.

"Hamilton wanted to show off, and let us see that he had money," said the captain, contemptuously. "I suppose we ought to vote him a medal—a gold one, studded with diamonds, seeing that he's a millionaire."

"That's not right, Ray," murmured Stiver in a low tone. "He's got us out of a hole."

"I don't care! I wish he'd take himself out of this academy. We don't want millionaires here."

Probably most of Dutton's feeling toward Dick, was due to jealousy, for Ray's father, though wealthy, was far from being as rich as Mr. Hamilton.

Dick bit his lip, to keep back a sharp reply at the unjust construction put upon his act.

"I shouldn't do anything for him again," whispered Paul.

"Well, I did it for the whole company, as much as for him," replied the young millionaire. "In another minute Colonel Masterly would have heard the row, and there'd been the mischief to pay."

The march was resumed after dinner and academy was reached in time for supper. The cadets were much pleased with their practice "hike," while the officers were complimented on the order they had maintained.

"I guess the colonel would preach a different sort of a sermon if he knew about the corn," remarked Paul, as he and Dick started for their quarters.

"Well, as long as he doesn't know, there's no harm done."

"My, but I'm tired," announced Paul, as he undressed. "I'm glad we don't have any lessons to-morrow."

"What do we have?"

"Artillery drill. Have you forgotten?"

"That's so. I had. I've got to ride one of the leading horses too. Guess there'll be plenty of excitement."

"Shouldn't wonder. I'm on the gun-carriage, where I reckon I'll be shaken so my liver pin will fall out."

"I'll try not to let it. There go taps. Douse the glim."

The two cadets crawled into bed and were soon asleep.

Artillery drill at the Kentfield academy was as near like the real article as possible. The guns were four-inch field pieces, each drawn by six horses, the two leaders being ridden by cadets, while seven men were on the gun itself, an arrangement somewhat different from that in the regular army. Real ammunition was used in practice, the pieces being directed at target placed against a hill of soft dirt, in which the balls buried themselves.

The artillery practice began soon after morning inspection. The cadets had all been instructed in how to load, aim and fire the field pieces, and had also had practice in driving the artillery into place. For the first time, however, they were now to indulge in this under the critical eye of an officer from the regular army, who was visiting the academy.

The first part of the drill consisted in firing at targets, before horses were hitched to the guns. The cadets did well at this, the different squads making good scores. Dick, who was detailed at the breech, had a chance to aim. He thought he sighted perfectly, but when it was fired the ball did not hit the target cleanly. It was the last shot in that particular part of the tactics, and it left Dick's squad with the lowest record.

"That's all your fault, Hamilton!" cried Captain Dutton angrily. "Why didn't you aim that right? Then we'd have had a chance to make a good score."

"I did aim it right, but the gun must have shifted. Maybe one of the wheels was on a small stone."

"Nonsense. It's your stupidity. You've lost us a good mark."

Dutton angrily slammed the breech-block shut. Dick gave a start, but stifled the cry of pain that he was ready to give utterance to, for one of his fingers was caught in the breech, and the blood spurted from it, as the angry captain closed the gun.

"Open the breech! Quick!" cried Paul, who had seen what had happened.

"What's that?" asked Dutton, who had turned aside.

Dick's roommate did not answer. Instead he took hold of the block with both hands, and wrenched it open, releasing our hero, whose white face showed the pain he suffered.

"Sorry I hurt you," said Dutton, calmly. "You shouldn't have had your finger there. I suppose you can't drive now, in the next test."

"I'll drive," said Dick, grimly, as he bound his handkerchief tightly around his finger, to stop the bleeding. The nail was smashed, and it was very painful.

"Then hurry up, and get the horses. They're ready to begin."

This test was a difficult one. In turn the different gun squads were to approach a certain spot on the gallop. They were to go through a narrow passage, indicated by stakes stuck into the ground, and, at the end were to suddenly wheel the gun, fire three shots, and continue on at a gallop to the end of the course. If any of the stakes were touched it counted against the squad, and other points were won or lost by the speed and accuracy of firing.

In spite of his pain Dick mounted his horse, and was soon ready, with 'Gene Graham, who was to ride the other steed, to start off with the field piece.

A squad from Company B went first. They cleared the stakes nicely, and did good work in wheeling and firing.

"I hope we beat them," murmured Captain Dutton, who was on the gun carriage.

Dick grimly resolved that if he had anything to do with it they would.

Company C's team came next, and did well, but the off horse struck a stake.

"Don't let that happen, Hamilton," cautioned Captain Dutton, as it came their turn.

Dick and Graham urged their animals to a gallop, and with a deep rumble the gun followed after them. On and on they went, toward the narrow lane formed by the upright stakes. Dick's heart was beating hard as he neared them. Would he clear them?

With unerring eye the young millionaire guided his animal, and so did Graham. With folded arms, and almost as stiff as ramrods, the cadets sat on the gun carriage. The leading horses were at the first stakes now, but the real test would come when the wide gun carriage reached them.

"Go on!" yelled Dick to his horse, a swift pace being most essential in order to keep on a straight course.

Dick gave a glance back. One wheel seemed about to hit a stake, but he quickly swerved his horse and the danger was averted. They got through without touching, and at a swifter pace than had any of their competitors. A burst of cheers from the watching cadets, and some visitors, rewarded them.

"Careful now!" cautioned Captain Dutton, as Dick wheeled his horse about.

Whether the animal was frightened at the cheering, or whether Dick, because of his injured finger, did not have a proper hold of the reins, was never known but, at that instant, the horse suddenly swerved, turning almost at right angles, and pulling off the course. So quickly was it done that it seemed as if the gun and carriage would upset, injuring several of the lads.

But Dick was equal to the occasion. Though the strain, which he had to put on the reins hurt his wounded hand very much, he never flinched. With a steady pull, and a sharp word of command, he swung his horse's head around, and just in time to avoid sending the gun over sideways.

Then, with a smart blow of his hand on the animal's flank Dick set him to a sharp gallop. Graham's steed, which had been pulled from his stride, regained it, and the horses behind, straightening out of the confusion into which they had been thrown, leaped forward, pulling the rumbling gun after them. Through it all, and in spite of their narrow escape, the cadets on the carriage had not so much as unfolded their arms.

On toward the place where they were to fire Dick and Graham rushed their horses. A moment later they wheeled them, the cadets leaped down, the gun was unlimbered, a shot rammed home, and the men stood at attention.

"Fire!" cried Captain Dutton.

A puff of white smoke, a sliver of flame and then a deep boom, while a black ball was hurled toward the distant target.

Twice more this was repeated, and then the gun was limbered, or attached to the limber, the forward part of the carriage, and the horses galloped off with it. Dick's squad had made a perfect score, in spite of the actions of his horse, and the cadets that came after them failed, so Captain Dutton's men won in the test.

But Dick felt sick and faint from the pain in his finger which had started to bleeding again, because of the strain caused by the reins.

CHAPTER XIV

CAPTAIN HANDLEE'S VISIT

"Very well done, young gentlemen—very well done indeed," complimented Colonel Masterly, as Dick and his fellow cadets came driving slowly past where the head of the academy sat with some visitors, and the army officer.

"Indeed, the regulars will have to look to their laurels when such lads as these are doing as well as that," observed the officer. "I thought they were going to have a spill there, at one time. But the lad on the off horse saved the day. Who is he?"

"Millionaire Hamilton's son," said the superintendent in a low voice, yet not so low but that Dick heard him.

"I wish they wouldn't refer to me that way," he thought. "I'd like to be myself once in a while—just Dick Hamilton. Money isn't what it's cracked up to be."

"Why, Hamilton, are you hurt?" asked Major Webster, as Dick guided his horse to the place where the animals would be unhitched. He looked at the red-stained handkerchief around the young millionaire's hand.

"Just a scratch," replied Dick bravely, though the pain of his crushed finger made him wince. "I caught it in the gun. It doesn't amount to anything."

He saw Dutton looking at him, and he fancied he detected a sneer on the cadet captain's face.

"Well, go to the surgeon, and have it dressed," said the major. "We don't want you to get blood poison. Is yours the only injury of the day?"

"I guess so," replied Dick, with an attempted laugh.

"A scratch!" exclaimed the surgeon, when Dick had so characterized the wound, as he came to have it dressed. "Well, I wouldn't want many scratches like that. Why the top of the finger is crushed. You shouldn't have kept on after you got this."

"I'd have to if we were fighting in earnest," was all Dick said, and he gritted his teeth hard to keep from screaming out when the surgeon dressed the wound.

Fortunately the remainder of the week was devoted to the more quieter forms of military life, the cadets spending considerable time in studying, drilling and reciting.

One afternoon word was sent to Dick, who was studying in his room, that a visitor desired to see him.

"Who is it?" he asked the housekeeper, who brought the message.

"I don't know. It's a gentleman from Hamilton Corners."

"I hope it's some of the boys," murmured Dick. "Or even a sight of 'Hank' Darby would be welcome," for, in spite of the activities at Kentfield, Dick was a bit homesick.

He found waiting for him Captain Handlee.

"I come to see if you had any news of my son," said the veteran pitifully. "I'm about to go out west on a clue I have, but I thought I'd stop off here."

"No," replied Dick, "I'm sorry, but I haven't any news for you. I wrote you about my inquiries."

"Yes, I know, but I hoped something might have happened since then."

"No, I regret to say, there hasn't. But how does it come that you're going out west?"

"Well, I have an idea I can get some clues there. I'm going to look up some old soldiers who were in my son's company. Your father gave me the money to go."

"My father? Is he home?" asked Dick quickly, hoping his parent had unexpectedly returned from abroad.

"Oh, no. He gave it to me before he left. I mentioned that I'd like to go out west, and he gave me a good sum. I don't know what I'd do but for him."

"When are you going west?" asked Dick.

"Right away. I guess I'd better be leaving here now."

"If you have any time to spare, captain, perhaps you'd like to stay and see the cadets go through some drills."

"I think I would, if the commander will let me."

"Of course he will. Old soldiers are always welcome here. We're going to have some wall-scaling drills just before parade this evening. I'd like to have you stay and see them."

"I will, thanks."

Dick spoke to Colonel Masterly about Captain Handlee, and the veteran not only received a cordial invitation to remain, but was taken in charge by Major Webster, who asked him to occupy his quarters, and take his meals there.

The wall-scaling drills were always enjoyed by the cadets as they offered chances for rough and ready fun. The walls were structures of boards, between ten and fifteen feet high, placed on the open field, and the object was for the lads, by means of a pyramid formation, to get all their comrades over the top, while the men left behind, who had assisted their fellows over, would either scramble up by means of a rope, anchored by lads on the other side, or would be pulled up by their comrades who leaned over the high fence.

CHAPTER XV

ON THE GRIDIRON

When the exercises for the day were over, Dick sought out Captain Handlee, and inquired how he liked the wall-scaling.

"Fine! Fine!" exclaimed the veteran. "We never had such practice when I was in the army, but we did pretty near the same in real life. I remember one occasion at Chancellorsville—"

"Now Captain Handlee," interrupted Major Webster, who had constituted himself host to the veteran, "you keep all such stories for me. If you get telling them to the cadets, first thing I know I'll have to be providing big brick walls for them to scale."

He led the veteran away, the aged captain bidding good-bye to Dick.

"I hope you'll be successful on your trip," said the young millionaire.

"I hope so, too, Dick, for I miss my son more and more as I grow older."

In spite of the good record he made in the drills, at artillery practice and in his class, Dick found as the weeks went by, that he was making no progress in becoming popular with the main body of students at Kentfield. He had a few chums among the freshmen, and of course was on speaking terms with all the others, but aside from Paul Drew, his roommate, he had no close friends. This state of affairs made him feel sad, for at home he had been the most popular lad in town.

"I'm not succeeding as I thought I would," he said to himself, one day. "I guess I'll have to put my plan into operation. But perhaps I'd better wait a while yet. I'll give this way a fair show."

As fall advanced there began to be talk about forming the football eleven. A number of new players were needed, because some of the best had graduated the previous year.

"I hope I can make the team," said Dick to Paul one evening during their study period. "I used to be considered a good player at home."

"I don't see why you can't get on. Fortunately Dutton has nothing to say about who shall play, though he's considered one of the team's supporters and backers."

"Still he may influence Captain Rutledge. I hear they are going to pick candidates this week."

"Yes, I heard Harry Hale, the coach, talking about it. I hope you make the eleven, Dick."

It was the following day, when Dick was out in the field, with some other cadets of his class, getting instruction in survey work, that he overheard something which made him feel more than ever like giving up the fight against his handicap. He was standing near a thick hedge, holding the scale rod, while another cadet was reading it through the instrument, when he heard voices behind the shrubbery.

"Looks to me like Hamilton would make a good player," he caught, and he knew that Coach Hale was speaking.

"You're right," said Captain Rutledge. "He's got the right build, and I hear he played at home."

"Aw, you don't want him on the team," expostulated a voice which Dick knew at once belonged to Captain Dutton.

"Why not?" asked the coach, in some surprise.

"Well, none of the other fellows like him. You wouldn't get good team work if he played."

"Are you sure?" asked Captain Rutledge.

"Sure. He's not popular."

"What's the matter with him?"

"Well, he's got too much money, and he's always trying to make it known. He gives himself as many airs as if he came of an old family."

This was an unjust accusation, but the coach and captain did not know it, as they were upper-class cadets, and did not mingle much with the freshmen.

"Well, we won't want to get an unpopular fellow on the eleven," said the coach, dubiously.

"No, indeed," agreed the captain. "Still, we need good players. Suppose we give him a trial?"

"You'll be sorry if you do," Dutton assured them.

Dick longed to drop the rod, leap over the hedge and give a well-deserved threshing to Dutton, but he knew he would lose more than he would gain. He was brought quickly out of his fit of righteous anger by the sharp command of the officer in charge of the surveying party.

"Plumb east there! Hamilton!" was the cry, and Dick saw that he had allowed the rod to slant too much. He straightened it, and, glancing at the hedge saw the three cadets who had been talking, moving away. But, before they got out of earshot Dick heard Dutton say:

"I wouldn't put him on the team, if I were you, for I don't think he'll be here long."

"Why not? Doesn't he like it?" asked Captain Rutledge.

"Oh, I guess he likes it all right, but we don't like him. I shouldn't wonder but what something would happen to make him leave," and Dutton laughed sarcastically.

"I guess I'd better be on my guard," thought Dick as he moved the rod to another place, in obedience to the instructions from the cadet at the instrument.

A few days after this, a notice was posted on the bulletin board in the gymnasium, telling all candidates for the football team to report on the gridiron that afternoon, as selections for the regular and scrub teams would be made. Members of the scrub would act as substitutes on the regular.

"Here's where I get my chance," said Dick to Paul.

"Well, I hope you make the regular team," replied his roommate, as the young millionaire went to submit himself for examination.

Coach Hale, Captain Rutledge, and a number of the former players were on hand, as was Dutton, and some of his cronies. All the candidates were looked over, sized up physically, and put through a course of "sprouts" in running, leaping, and tackling. Then their football history was inquired into.

"I guess you'll do, Hamilton," said the coach, and Dick was delighted.

A moment later, however, he saw his hopes dashed to the ground. Dutton called Harry Hale over to him, whispered a bit, and then Captain Rutledge joined them.

"You'll be on the scrub, Hamilton," said Hale, a little later. "You'll probably have a chance to play in several games, however, for I like your form. You've got to be regular at practice however."

Though much disappointed, Dick vowed to do his best at practice. This was started a few days later, and, when the regular team lined up against the substitutes, Dick resolved that theywould make no gains through him, for he was playing at left guard, though he preferred being back of the line.

"Well, how are we making out," Dick overheard Captain Rutledge asking the coach, one afternoon, following some hard scrimmages.

"Pretty good. That Hamilton is like a brick wall, though. We can't gain a foot through him. I wish we had him on the regular."

"Well, you know what Dutton said."

"Yes, I know, but I don't believe all Dutton says. He's got queer notions. I think Hamilton is every bit as good as he is. Besides, Dutton doesn't play football."

"I know it, but he has lots of influence."

Dick fully subscribed to this, for he knew it was due to Dutton that he was on the scrub instead of on the regular team. But he resolved to have patience.

As Dick walked off the gridiron, following the practice, he was met, before he reached his barracks, by Grit, who had been let out of his kennel in the stables.

"Hello, Grit old fellow!" exclaimed Dick, and the dog nearly dislocated his stump of a tail, so excited was he. Since rejoining his master he had picked up wonderfully. "I've got you for a friend, even if I haven't many others," said Dick, as he bent over to fondle the dog. As he did so he saw some marks on the animal's smooth, satin-like coat, that made him start.

"Grit, you've been fighting!" he exclaimed. "How did that happen?" He knew there were no other dogs near the academy with whom his pet would quarrel. He asked the stableman about it.

"Sure Grit's been in a fight," replied one of the hostlers. "I thought you matched him in a scrap wid a dorg in town. Grit won, anyhow. It was a couple a' nights ago."

"Matched him in a fight? Why, did some one—some of the cadets take Grit to town, and let him fight?"

"Thot's what they done, Muster Hamilton, an' they won a pot of money on him too, I understand."

"Who took him?" asked Dick, trying to speak calmly.

"Why, uts no secret. Muster Dutton an' Muster Stiver tuck him one night. Ut was a foin foight, I heard 'em say."

Dick started away, after chaining Grit up, a set look on his face.

"I'll have it out with Dutton," he said.

CHAPTER XVI

FOR THE PRIZE TROOP

After a bath and rub down in the gymnasium Dick dressed for evening parade. When this was over he sought out Dutton, who was strolling off the campus with some chums.

"Captain Dutton, I wish to speak to you," said Dick, formally saluting.

"Well, I don't know that I wish to speak to you. What is it?" asked the young snob, barely acknowledging Dick's courtesy.

"Did you take my bulldog to town, and match him to fight another?"

Dutton started, then looked insolently at Dick.

"What of it?" he asked sneeringly.

"This much. That you haven't any right to do that, even if you are my superior officer. Grit is my personal property, and I won't have him fighting."

"Aw, what's the harm, Hamilton. He put up a dandy fight and licked a bigger dog than he is," put in one of the cadets.

"I don't care, I don't want him to fight."

"Oh, you don't?" asked Dutton coolly.

"No; and if you take him again——"

"Well, what will you do? Report me, I suppose?" said the captain.

"No, but I'll thrash you worse than I did the other time, Captain Dutton, that's what I'll do!" exclaimed Dick, hotly. "You leave Grit alone! If you take him again you know what to expect!"

Dutton turned pale. He strode toward Dick, but at that moment Captain Grantly, one of the instructors, strolled past. Dutton turned aside.

"You haven't heard the last of this—my fresh millionaire," he said in a whisper to Dick, as he and his cronies walked off. "You'll wish you hadn't insulted me."

Dick saluted, as the rules required, and marched back to quarters. He felt that he would have enjoyed a good stiff fight with his mean enemy.

"I don't suppose this will add to my popularity, among the sporting element," he said to himself. "But I don't care; they shan't fight Grit!"

Football practice went on every afternoon, and Dick and the other scrubs were faithful at it. The regular eleven was being whipped into shape, and the first game was close at hand. When it was played Dick found himself wishing he could have a chance, but no such thing happened. The opponents of Kentfield were light-weight players, and the cadets had no difficulty in piling up a big score.

"But it will be different next week," Captain Rutledge warned them. "We tackle Mooretown then, and you'll find your work cut out for you."

This game was indeed a stiff one, and several players were hurt. The cadets were slightly ahead in the second half, when the right half-back was knocked out, and, as there had been one substitute already put in at that position, there was a call for another one.

"Try Hamilton," suggested the coach, after a hurried consultation with the captain.

Dick's heart gave a wild throb, as he was called, and, stripping off his sweater, he bounded in from the side line. He was given the ball for a play around the left end, and, getting clear of the opposing players started down the field on a run. But, alas for his hopes of making a touchdown! The referee's whistle blew when he was on the thirty-five yard line, ending the game, in favor of Kentfield.

There was rejoicing among the cadets, for Mooretown was an ancient rival, and they played three games with the students of that non-military academy every year, for the local championship.

"You didn't get much of a show, Hamilton," said Coach Hale, as the team was in the dressing room. "But you started off well. I guess you'll get into a game yet."

Dick was grateful for this praise. He knew he could do good work if he had half a chance.

"This is Saturday," observed Paul Drew, as he crawled out of bed the next morning. "Not so many lessons to-day, and lots of fun for you, I suppose on the horses. It's rough-riding to-day."

"So it is," agreed Dick. "I like that best of all, except, maybe, hiking on a practice march, and firing from the trenches. I hope I get the horse I had last time."

"To-day's the last of the tests," went on Paul, as he slipped into his uniform.

"How do you mean?"

"I mean the officers are going to choose from those who ride to-day, the cadets who can take part in the tests for joining the prize troop."

"Right you are. Say, I'm going to make that troop or bust a leg."

"Well, I hope you don't break any bones. But I guess there's no danger. You seem right at home on a horse."

"I ought to. I've been riding ever since I was a kid. I'm going to do my best to-day."

As Paul had said, this was the final weeding out of candidates among the cadets, who had no chance in the tests that would be held later, to determine who should be members of the prize troop. This troop consisted of the best riders at the academy, and took part in several state evolutions and parades, having won a number of trophies.

Scores of cadets, in their service uniforms, reported on the cavalry plain for practice. They were required to vault into the saddle while their horse was standing still, and at varying speeds, up to a smart gallop. Many failed in this, but Dick did not.

Then came mounting and dismounting at hurdles, which was more difficult, and weeded out a number, and then, the last of the semifinals, was the feat of standing astride on two horses, driving a steed on either side, and, while doing this, to take a difficult hurdle.

More than a score did not succeed at this, and Dick was not a little nervous when it came his turn, as, though he was an expert, he had not practiced this evolution much.

On his steeds thundered over the ground, one being a skittish horse, and hard to manage.

"If they don't jump together," thought Dick, "I'm done for. If one of them knocks down the hurdle bar it's all up with my chances."

He called encouragingly to the animals, and took a tighter hold on the reins, while he shifted his weight on the backs of the horses.

"Over you go now, boys!" he exclaimed at the take-off, and he fairly lifted the four animals as one, over the bar, clearing it cleanly.

"Good, Hamilton!" was the quiet praise of Major Webster, who acted as judge. "That was finely done."

So Dick qualified for the finals.

But there was more hard work ahead of him. Thus far not many of the freshmen had kept up to Dick, and there were envious eyes cast at him. But those who envied him his good fortune realized that he had earned it.

"Now, gentlemen, ready for the finals," ordered Major Webster. "I want you all to be careful, and take no unnecessary risks, at the same time, don't be afraid, for no one ever became a good horseman who was afraid."

The final tests consisted in riding bareback, in different postures, such as might become necessary during a battle, in riding at different speeds, in removing the saddle from the horse while at full gallop, in leaping hurdles, and taking water jumps.

Other tests were in leaping hurdles four feet high, and as the cadets vaulted, taking a suspending ring on a lance, in leaping clean over a running horse and in forming pyramids, with ten cadets on four horses.

The last test was, perhaps, the most difficult of all. It consisted in one cadet lying on the ground, and another riding toward him at full speed. The one on the horse had to pick up his comrade from the earth, by leaning over and grasping his up-stretched hand, and then assisting him up behind him on his horse, continuing to gallop away.

When it came Dick's turn he noticed, with some uneasiness, that the cadet he was to pick up, was one of the heaviest in the school, but he resolved to succeed, and he braced himself for the ordeal, as his horse galloped toward the prostrate youth.

As he neared the recumbent figure Dick leaned over, holding on as tightly as he could with his legs. His hand grasped the belt and part of the clothing of the cadet, and then Dick's arm felt as if it would be torn from the socket. He feared he would be dragged from his horse.

But, with a sudden pull, he lifted the lad from the ground and swung him upon his horse. There was some applause at Dick's feat, as his steed galloped on over the course.

"Guess I'm something of a load, old chap," said the cadet to Dick.

"You're no feather," was Dick's comment, as he halted his horse.

CHAPTER XVII

DICK IN TROUBLE

"Well, Hamilton, I think we shall admit you to membership in the prize troop," said Major Webster. "It was a severe test, and you did well."

"I'm glad you think so, sir," replied Dick, saluting.

There were some further trials, in some of them Dick acting the part of the reclining cadet. 'Gene Graham could not succeed in the test, and was rejected, much to his disappointment.

Dick was delighted to be a member of the prize troop for it brought with it many privileges; and there was a chance to take part in parades and similar affairs to which the other cadets were not admitted.

Very few freshmen had won the coveted honor, but it can not be said that Dick was received with open arms into the troop. Dutton and many of his friends belonged, and they had lost none of their unreasonable feeling against Dick. Still they did nothing more than turn a cold shoulder toward him, though this was enough to make the young millionaire miserable.

However, he managed to forget some of his bad feeling in anticipation of another football game, which was to take place two days later. He hoped to get a chance to play, as, following a rather tame affair with a team which the Kentfield eleven "walked all over," there was to be the second of the championship contests with Mooretown.

This was a lively and strenuous game. Mooretown put in some new players, and, though they did not score in the first half, when Kentfield made one touchdown, the opponents of the cadet warriors of the gridiron took such a brace in the second that the score was ten to four, in favor of Mooretown, when the referee's whistle blew.

"What's the matter with your men?" asked Coach Hale of Captain Rutledge, after the game. "They couldn't hold those fellows for a cent."

"Too much beef for us," replied the captain.

"Yes, and they tore holes in your line that you could drive an ice wagon through," went on the coach. "Both your guards were weak. Hamilton should have been put in."

"I couldn't very well do it, when no men were hurt."

"No, I suppose not. But if the next game doesn't go better than this one did, I'll make a change. We can't afford to lose it."

"We shan't lose it," promised the captain, and Dick, who overheard what was said, hoped he would get a chance to play.

Meanwhile he reported regularly for practice, and was a tower of strength to the scrub eleven, many of the players on which, regardless of Dutton's influence, made of Dick a better friend than heretofore.

Several unimportant games followed, one of which resulted in a tie, Kentfield winning the others, and then came the occasion of the final struggle with Mooretown. It was the greatest game of the season, as it meant much to both academies.

The day before the contest Dick was surprised to receive a visit from Russell Glen, one of the freshmen cadets, who, hitherto, had scarcely taken the trouble to nod to him. Glen wanted to be considered a "sport," and Dick had heard that he had had a hand in taking Grit off to the dog fight.

"I had a letter from a friend of mine to-day," said Glen, by way of introduction, as he lolled in one of Dick's easy chairs. "It contained some surprising news."

"Yes?" asked Dick politely.

"Yes, it was from Guy Fletcher, of Hamilton Corners. He spoke of you, and asked me if I knew you."

"Well?" asked Dick, wondering what was coming.

"I was quite surprised to know that you and Guy were friends," went on Glen.

"Oh, yes, I've known Guy for some time," said Dick, not caring to go into particulars, and tell what a mean trick Guy, in company with Simon Scardale, had once played on him.

"So he says. He speaks very highly of you. I've known him for some time. He and I used to be quite chummy. But I had no idea you and he lived in the same town, until he spoke of it in his letter. He mentioned that you attended this academy, and asked if I was acquainted with you. I wrote back and said that I was."

Dick looked rather surprised at this, as well he might, for, beyond a mere nod, Glen had never shown that he knew him.

"I don't suppose I am as well acquainted with you as I might be," went on the young "sport," calmly, "and that's my fault. I've been so busy attending to my studies, that I haven't had much time for social calls."

Neither had many of the other cadets, Dick thought bitterly.

"But I'll make amends now," went on Glen. "I want to get to know you better, because we both have the same friend in Guy Fletcher."

Dick didn't think it worth while to state that Guy was no particular friend of his, since certain happenings told of in the first volume of this series. But Glen continued:

"I wish you'd come to a little spread I'm giving to-night. Just a small affair for some of the freshmen."

"I'll come," promised our hero, glad of the chance to meet some of his classmates informally.

"It won't be as elaborate as the one I hear you gave," went on Glen, "for I'm not a millionaire," and he laughed. "But I'll do the best I can."

At first Dick thought he was going to have a good time at the affair, for the guests, most of whom were of the "sporting" element, greeted him cordially enough. But when Glen produced several bottles of beer, and some cigars, Dick felt uneasy.

It was an offense, calling for severe punishment, to have intoxicants or tobacco in the academy, and Dick realized that discovery might come any moment. Still, he did not want to bring upon himself ridicule, and perhaps anger, by leaving.

"Have some beer, Hamilton," urged Glen.

"It's the right sort of stuff. I had it smuggled in from town. And these are prime cigars. I snibbled some from dad's stock before I came away."

"No, thank you," replied Dick. "I don't care for any."

"What, don't you drink?"

"No."

"Aw, you don't know what life is. Have a cigar then."

"No, I don't smoke, either."

"Humph! You're a regular molly-coddle, you are," said Glen, with a brutal laugh.

Dick flushed.

"Maybe," he admitted, as pleasantly as he could, "but I have an idea I shouldn't drink or smoke while in training, if for no other reason."

"Your training doesn't seem to be doing you much good," said another cadet. "You haven't had a show in any of the games yet. Better quit training and have some beer."

"No, thank you. Maybe I'll get a chance to play to-morrow."

But Dick's refusal had no effect on Glen's other guests. They drank more than was good for them, and smoked considerable. They were becoming rather noisy and silly, and Dick was in momentary terror lest some guard or instructor should come along and discover the violation of the rules. The spread was held in an unused room, in the basement of the east barrack, and, though permission for it had been given, the officer in charge of the building was supposed to keep a sort of lookout over such affairs.

If one of the cadet officers discovered the beer and cigars he would hardly "squeal" on his comrades, but one of the academy staff would not be so lenient.

The fun became more and more noisy, and Dick was thinking of withdrawing, no matter if he did offend his host, when he was saved the trouble by something that happened.

A cadet officer, who was on night guard knocked on the door, and when there came a sudden hush to the merry-making, he whispered that Major Webster was approaching, and would almost certainly discover the breach of rules.

"Quick fellows, get this stuff out of the way, and then skip!" cried Glen, and the boys quickly hid the beer bottles, and threw away their cigars. Then, by opening the windows, the smoke was gotten rid of, and the cadets prepared to disperse.

"I say, Hamilton," began Glen, a bit thickly, as he walked alongside Dick, to his room, "you couldn't lend me twenty-five dollars; could you? I spent more on this racket than I intended, and I'm a bit short until I get my next allowance. I want to bet a little on the game to-morrow."

"I guess I can let you have it," said Dick good naturedly. "Come to my room, and I'll get it."

It was after ten o'clock, but as Dick had received permission to attend the spread, he had a permit to be out after taps. Paul, who had not been invited, was asleep when Dick and Glen entered.

"I say, Hamilton, you keep your room looking nice," said the "sport" as he looked around the neat apartment. "I'm always getting a mark at police inspection, for having something out of kilter. You and Drew are as neat as girls."

"Hush! Not so loud," cautioned Dick. "You'll wake, Paul."

"Aw, what's the odds. He'll go to sleep again. It's early yet. Be a sport!"

Glen was noisy from the beer which he had taken.

"Here is the money," said Dick, handing over some bills.

"Thanks, old chap. I'll see that you get it back all right."

"There's no hurry."

"All right; if I win, though, I'll pay you to-morrow. Do you think we'll lick Mooretown?"

"I hope so. But you'd better go to bed now."

"Me? Go to bed? Wha' for?"

"Well, it's getting late, and some one might come along. You'd better go."

"That's a' right. I'm goin'. You're a' right, Ham'ton. You're a' right. You're sport!"

And, rather unsteady on his legs, poor, foolish Glen went away, much to Dick's relief.

"I don't much care for friends, such as he is," thought Dick, as he got into bed.

In his generousness it never occurred to him that Glen had cultivated his acquaintance merely that he might borrow money from him.

Dick was awakened by the clear, sweet notes of the bugle sounding reveille. He and Paul jumped out of bed, and were soon in their uniforms. Then they got their room in order for police inspection, which, on some days, was made while they were at breakfast. This was one of those occasions.

"There, I guess they can't find any fault with that," observed Dick, as he and his roommate, putting the finishing touches to their apartment, descended to form in line to march to the mess hall.

Dick was leaving the table, to attend chapel, when Cadet Captain Naylor, who was in charge of the police inspection, tapped him on the shoulder.

"Hamilton, report to Major Rockford," he said curtly.

"To Major Rockford? What for?"

"Room out of order."

"Room out of order?"

Dick knew that he and Paul had left their apartment in perfect trim.

But Captain Naylor did not answer, and Dick, with a heavy heart, started for the commandant's office. It was the first time he had been made to report for a breach of discipline of this sort.

CHAPTER XVIII

A DISMAL CHRISTMAS

"You are reported as not having your room in order, Hamilton," began Major Rockford, as Dick entered.

"I don't see how that can be, sir," replied Dick, saluting. "When Paul Drew and I left it for breakfast it was in order."

"Drew's side is yet, but your bureau is stated by Captain Naylor to be in great disorder."

"I—I left it in order, sir."

"Very well, we will go and take a look at it."

Accompanied by the commandant, Dick went to his apartment. To his surprise his neat bureau was in great disorder, the objects on it being scattered all about.

"Well?" asked Major Rockford.

"Some one—some one must have been in here, sir," said Dick.

"Ha! Do you wish to accuse any one?"

Dick went closer to his bureau. Something on it caught his eye. It was a note written in pencil. It read:

"Dear Hamilton: I am awfully sick this morning. I lost that twenty-five you loaned me. Can you let me have some more? I called but you were out, so I wrote this note here. Please let me have the money.

"Russell Glen."

Then Dick understood. Glen, suffering from the effects of his dissipation the night before, had called at the room after our hero and Paul had left to go to breakfast. In writing the note Glen had, probably unthinkingly, disarranged the things on Dick's bureau, where he wrote and left the missive. Then he had gone away, and, Captain Naylor, on police inspection, had seen the disorder, and reported Dick.

"Do you wish to accuse any one?" went on Major Rockford.

Dick thought rapidly. To tell the true circumstances, and show Glen's note, would mean that the facts of the spread would come out. Glen and his chums would be punished, and Dick might be censured. It would be better to accept the blame for having his room in disorder, rather than incur the displeasure of his comrades by being the means of informing on Glen.

So Dick answered:

"I—I guess I was mistaken, sir. I am sorry my room was out of order."

"So am I, Hamilton, for you have a good record. Still there have been several violations of late, among the cadets, and I must make an example. But, in view of your good conduct, and record I will not give you any demerits."

"Thank you, sir."

"Still, I must inflict some punishment You will not be allowed to attend the football game this afternoon, but must remain in your room."

That was punishment indeed, for Dick felt that he would have a chance to play. Still, like a good soldier, he did not murmur. He concealed Glen's note in his hand, saluted the major and then, as chapel was over, he marched to his classroom, with a heavy heart.

"I wonder if that was part of a plot to get me into trouble," thought Dick, as he recalled what he had overheard Dutton say. "They're trying to force me to leave the academy. But I'll not go! I'll fight it out!"

He felt very lonesome as he had to retire to his room that afternoon, and heard the merry shouts of the football eleven, the substitutes, and the other cadets leaving for the final battle on the gridiron with Mooretown.

"How I wish I could go!" thought Dick. "I'm punished for something I didn't do. It isn't right. Still, perhaps Glen was so sick he didn't know what he was doing."

He had already sent Glen some more money, for he did not want to refuse one of the few favors that had been asked of him since coming to the academy.

As he was moping in his room, Toots came along, whistling "Three Cheers for the Red, White and Blue," and giving a succession of bugle calls.

"What? Not at the game, Mister Hamilton?" asked the jolly janitor.

"No; I'm a prisoner."

"That's nothing. Many a time I got out of the guard house. There's no one around now, and I won't look, nor squeal. You can easily slip out, and go to the game."

"No," said Dick, though the temptation was strong. "By the way, Toots, did you ever call to mind about this picture?" and he showed him the one of missing Bill Handlee, which was still on the mantle.

"No," replied Toots, again striving hard to remember about it. "It's clean gone from me, Mr. Hamilton. But, are you sure you don't want to escape? I can find some work to do at the other side of the barracks, if you want to go."

"No. I'll stay."

And stay Dick did, all that long afternoon. It was dusk when the players and the other cadets came back, and there was an ominous silence about their return.

"It doesn't sound as if they'd won," thought Dick. "If they did they're celebrating very quietly."

Paul Drew came in a little later.

"How about the game?" asked Dick eagerly.

"We lost," said Paul. "We might have won, only Henderson, who had a chance to score a winning touchdown, couldn't run fast enough with the ball, and he was downed on the five-yard line, too late for another try to cross the Mooretown goal. I wish you had played. You'd have won the game for us."

"Oh, I guess not."

"Yes, you would. Captain Rutledge admitted as much."

"Well, maybe I'll get a chance next time."

"There won't be any next time this year. The game is over for the season, and Mooretown did us two contests out of three. It's too bad. The fellows are all cut up over it. Say, have you any idea who mussed up your bureau? Was it Dutton?"

"No, it wasn't Dutton," said Dick quietly, and that was all he could be induced to say about it.

Discipline, which had been somewhat relaxed during the football season, was now in force again, and the cadets found they were kept very busy with their studies and drills. Dick was standing well in his classes, but he made no more progress in gaining the friendship of the students, other than a few freshmen.

Even Glen showed no disposition to make much of Dick. He did not repay the money borrowed, on the plea that he was in debt quite heavily, and had lost much on the football game. Still he had the cheek to ask Dick for more, and when the young millionaire properly refused Glen called him a "tight-wad," and sneered at him, making no pretense of retaining his friendship.

One night, following several spreads, to none of which was Dick invited, he wrote a rather discouraged letter to his father, hinting that he wished he could attend some other school.

In due time there came an answer, part of which was as follows:

"You know the terms were that you were to remain at least a full term. Still, if you do not wish to, you have the choice of going to your Uncle Ezra. He will send you to a boarding school of his own selection. Let me know what you will do. I will not be able to get home by Christmas, as I expected, and you had better remain at the academy over the holidays. I know it will be lonesome for you, but it can't be helped."

"Go to a boarding school selected by Uncle Ezra," murmured Dick. "Never! I'll stay here a full term, even if no one but the teachers speak to me. I never could stand Uncle Ezra and Dankville. This is bad enough, but there are some bright spots in it. The sun never shines where Uncle Ezra is."

Yet the time was coming when Uncle Ezra was to do Dick a great favor, though he himself was not aware of it.

So Dick sent word to his father that he would remain at Kentfield. Fall merged into winter, and overcoats were the order of the day at all out-door exercises. Much of the drilling and parading was omitted, and more study and recitation was indulged in. What maneuvers on horseback and afoot were held, took place mainly in the big riding hall or drill room, and they were not as attractive as when held out of doors.

"Well, are you going home for Christmas?" asked Paul, about a week before the holiday vacation.

"Guess not," replied Dick, somewhat gloomily. "Our house is shut up, and I don't care about spending Christmas at a hotel in Hamilton Corners."

"Come home with me."

"No, thank you. I was thinking of visiting some of my chums at home. I believe I'll do that. I'll be glad to see them again."

Dick knew he would be welcomed at the homes of any of his friends, and he planned to go to Hamilton Corners and surprise them.

But alas for his hopes! When the last day of school came, and the other cadets made hurried preparations to leave for home, poor Dick was taken with a heavy cold. The surgeon forbade him leaving his room, as the weather was cold and stormy, and our hero was forced to remain at Kentfield, in charge of the housekeeper and the doctor, while the other cadets joyfully departed to happy firesides.

"Sorry to leave you, old chap," said Paul, sympathetically, "but my folks wouldn't know what to do if I didn't come home over the holidays."

"That's all right," said Dick, hoarsely, but as cheerfully as he could. "I'll see you after New Year's. Have a good time."

"I will. Hope you get better."

It was a gloomy Christmas for the young millionaire, and, as a fever set in with his cold, he couldn't even enjoy the good things which the kind housekeeper, under orders from Colonel Masterly, provided for the patient.

The academy was a very lonely place indeed, Christmas day, for all the officers and cadets had gone, leaving only the housekeeper, and some of the janitors, including Toots, in charge.

Dick received some tokens from abroad, sent by his father, and a cheery letter, which he answered in the same strain.

"But it isn't much like Christmas," thought Dick, as he sat up in bed. Then a bright thought came to him.

"Can't Toots have dinner up here with me?" he asked Mrs. Fitzpatrick.

"Of course he can," she said. "Maybe it will cheer you up," and she sent for the jolly janitor.

CHAPTER XIX

THE MARKSMAN MEDAL

Toots' advance along the corridor leading to Dick's room was announced by his rendering of the tune "The Star Spangled Banner," which he ended with a spirited bugle call.

"Did you send for me, Mr. Hamilton?" he asked as he came in.

"I did, Toots," said Dick. "I thought maybe you would like to have dinner with me here. I'm lonesome, and I suppose you are, too."

"Bless your heart, not exactly lonesome, Mr. Hamilton, but I'm glad to come just the same. You see I'm too busy to be lonesome. I've got lots to do, cleaning up all the rooms against the cadets coming back in a couple of weeks."

"Then maybe you haven't time to spend an hour or so here."

"Oh, I reckon I have. But it's agin the regulations for me to eat here. I'm supposed to eat with the other servants."

"We'll make our own regulations for the time being," said Dick. "Here comes Mrs. Fitzpatrick with the grub. I hope you're hungry, for I'm not particularly."

"Well, I can eat a bit," admitted Toots. "I say, though, that is a spread!" he exclaimed, as he saw the good things the housekeeper was bringing into Dick's room, where she set them on a table.

"Well, it's Christmas," observed Dick, "though I can't eat much myself. However, it'll do me good to see you put it away."

"And I can do that same," admitted Toots cheerfully.

Dick, under the doctor's orders was allowed only a bit of the white meat of the turkey, and none of the "stuffing," so he could not make a very substantial meal, but Toots ate enough for three.

"I don't suppose you got this sort of thing in the army," ventured Dick, wishing to have his odd friend talk somewhat of his experiences, for he had learned that Toots had once been janitor at a military post.

"No, indeed," replied Toots. "We did get a little extra at holiday times, but nothing like this."

"How did you come to be at the military post?" asked Dick.

"Blessed if I know. I was always a sort of a rover, and I suppose I wandered out west. I'm going to join the army some time. I'm a good shot, you know. Did you ever see me shoot?"

"Yes," replied Dick, trying not to smile, as he thought of how far Toots had come from hitting the target.

"Yes, I'm a good shot," went on the janitor. "But I'm going to improve. I'll practice on the range this winter at odd times. You're a pretty good shot yourself, ain't you?"

"Fair," admitted Dick, as he watched Toots put away the roast turkey and the "fixings."

"A-ker-choo!" suddenly sneezed Toots, pulling out his handkerchief. "Aker-choo-choo! Guess I put too much pepper on my potatoes," he said.

Something fell to the floor, as Toots pulled out his handkerchief. It lay in sight of Dick, who was propped up in bed.

"What's that?" he asked. "You dropped something."

The man picked it up, and Dick saw that it was a marksman's bronze medal.

"Let me see that," he said, quickly, and the janitor passed it over.

"Why this was given to some soldier, for good shooting," went on our hero, as he tried to decipher the name on it. "Where did you get it, Toots?"

"Blessed if I know, Mr. Hamilton. I've had it a long time. It was given to me by some friend, I expect. I found it the other day in my trunk. I'd forgotten I had it. But if it's a marksman's badge, I'm going to wear it. I'm a good shot."

Dick looked more closely at it. Besides the name of some soldier the badge contained the name of the command to which he had belonged, but everything save the letters "mie, Wyo." were obliterated by dents and scratches.

A sudden thought came to Dick. It was in connection with Toot's half-recognition of the picture of missing Bill Handlee. It was evident that Toots knew something of the captain's son, but he could not straighten out the kink in his memory, and possibly this marksman's badge might be a clue. Dick hoped so, and he decided to try to learn from what fort or command the medal had been given.

"I wish you'd let me take this for a few days, Toots," he said. "I'll take good care of it."

"All right, Mr. Hamilton, but don't lose it. If it's what you say it is, I'm going to wear it, to show I'm a good shot. Then I won't have to be telling people all the while. They can see it for themselves."

"Can't you recollect where you got it?" asked Dick again.

Toots shook his head.

"It's like—like the time you asked me about his picture," he said, pointing to the photo on the mantle. "I get all sort of confused in my head. Maybe I always had it. Maybe someone gave it to me when I was janitor at the fort out west."

"What fort was that?"

"I've forgotten. It's a good while ago. But don't lose that medal, Mr. Hamilton. I'm going to wear it."

"Poor Toots," thought Dick. "All the medals in the world will never make you a good shot."

He put the badge carefully away, resolving to ask Major Webster, at the first opportunity, from what military post it was likely to have come.

Thanks to the jolly companionship of Toots, Christmas was not as gloomy as Dick had feared it would be. The dinner over the janitor left Dick to himself, and our hero fell into a refreshing sleep. When he awoke he felt much better, and the doctor said he could be out in a couple of days, if the weather moderated.

The first of the year dawned; a fine bracing day, and, as there was no biting wind, Dick was allowed to stroll about the campus a short time. This brought the color to his cheeks, and completed the cure begun by the surgeon's medicine.

"Well, things will be lively a week from to-night," said Toots one day, as he came in to make up Dick's room.

"Why?"

"The boys will be back then. Vacation will be over."

"I'm glad of it," commented Dick, and then, with pain in his heart, he wondered if the coming term would bring him more fellowship than had the preceding one.

Major Webster was among the first of the instructors to arrive, in anticipation of the return of the students, and to him Dick showed the medal.

"Why, yes; that's one given out years ago, at Fort Laramie, Wyoming," he said. "I can send it to a friend of mine for you, if you like. Possibly they may be able to trace the illegible name from the fort records."

"I wish you would," said Dick. "Maybe I can get a trace of Captain Handlee's son for him."

"I doubt it," replied the major, shaking his head. "I tried all the sources of information I knew, and it was useless. Still you may have better luck."

The medal was sent off, but, fearing nothing would come of it, Dick did not say anything to Captain Handlee about it, though he wrote to the veteran in answer to a letter the old soldier sent him.

The holiday vacation came to a close, and, one morning Dick awoke to a realization that, on that day, the cadets would come pouring back.

It was nearly noon when the first of them arrived. Among them was Paul Drew.

"Well, how are you, old chap?" he cried, rushing into Dick's room.

"Pretty good. How about you?"

"Oh, I had a dandy time, home. I almost hated to come back, but I wanted to see you, and then I know we'll have some sport this winter. Say, there are a lot of new fellows. We're not so fresh as we were. There are others. There's going to be hazing to-night, I understand. Thank fortune they won't bother me. I don't fancy cold water down my back on a winter night."

"Hazing, eh?" remarked Dick. And he wondered if his turn would come.

CHAPTER XX

DICK DOESN'T TELL

All the rest of that day cadets continued to arrive at Kentfield Academy, and there were lively scenes on the snow-covered campus, in the assembly auditoriums, students' rooms, and in the mess hall.

Several new cadets stood about, looking rather miserable, Dick thought, and he spoke to some of them, telling them where to report, and what to do, for he appreciated what it meant to be a stranger among a lot of lads who ignored new-comers, not because they were heartless so much as that they were thoughtless.

Dick rather hoped Dutton would not return, but that cadet was among the first he encountered as he strolled over the white campus.

Dutton nodded coolly, and Dick as coolly acknowledged the bow. Then Dutton saw a freshman standing near the saluting cannon. It was one of the unwritten rules of the school that none below the grade of sophomores might stand near the cannon.

"Here, fresh!" cried Dutton roughly, "stand away from that gun!"

The lad, a small chap, did not seem to comprehend.

Dick put in a word.

"You can't stand near there until you're a second year," he told the lad. "It's a school rule, that's all."

"I say, Hamilton, I guess I can manage my own affairs," said Dutton, angrily. "You mind your own business; will you?"

"I guess I've got as much right to speak as you have," said Dick hotly. "I was only telling him what to do."

The freshman looked from one to the other. Quite a group had gathered by this time, attracted by Dutton's loud voice. The new lad moved a short distance away from the gun.

"Don't you know enough to mind when you're spoken to?" demanded Dutton, advancing toward him. "I'll teach you manners, you young cub! Why don't you salute when an officer speaks to you? Now get back," and, with that he gave the lad such a shove that he went over backward into a snow bank, made by shoveling the white crystals away from the gun.

"That's not right, Dutton!" exclaimed Dick.

"You mind your own affairs, or I'll do the same to you, Hamilton," retorted the bully.

"You'd better try it," said Dick quietly. "If you want to fight with me, you know what to do. Just lay a finger on me."

He took a step toward his enemy, and stood waiting for him. But Dutton knew better than to attack Dick. He had felt the weight of his fists once, and he knew he had no chance in a fair fight.

So he strode away, muttering to the lad whom he had knocked down:

"You keep away from this gun, after this, fresh."

Dick did not think it wise to say anything further on the side of the mistreated one. Already he saw some unpleasant looks directed toward him by Dutton's friends, and he realized that by interfering in what was considered one of the rights of upper classmen, to assume a bullying attitude toward those in the lower grades, he was not adding to his popularity. I am glad to say that such characters as Dutton were in the small majority at Kentfield, and that though some of his cronies applauded his action in knocking the newcomer down, most of the lads were not in sympathy with the bully.

But there were so many things occurring, so many cadets arriving, some of whom wanted to change their apartments, to get new roommates, or be quartered in other sections of the barracks, that all was in seeming confusion.

Colonel Masterly and his aides, however, had matters well in hand, and by night, when the cadets lined up for the march to mess, affairs were in some sort of order.

"Do you want to make a shift, Paul?" asked Dick, as they went to their room early that evening.

"A shift? What do you mean?"

"Why some of your friends have changed over to the east barrack, I hear. I thought maybe you'd want to go too?"

"Do you want me to go?"

"Indeed I don't!" and Dick spoke very earnestly.

"All right. When I want to leave you I'll let you know," and Paul slapped Dick on the back in a fashion that told what his feelings were in the matter.

A little later mysterious steps in the corridor, and subdued knockings on nearby doors told Paul and Dick that something unusual was going on.

"Hazing," said Paul. "We're immune. Let's take it in."

"I don't like to haze fellows," said Dick. "It's all right when they're your size, but all the chaps who came in lately are smaller than I am."

"That won't make any difference to Dutton and his crowd. They'll haze 'em anyhow, and we might as well see the fun. A fellow who can't stand a little hazing is no good."

"That's so. Guess I'll go. I don't mind it if it isn't too rough. I wouldn't mind being hazed myself. It would give me a chance to make a rough house for Dutton and his cronies."

"Come on then. Let's go to the gym. I heard that they're going to haze a bunch of 'em there."

"What about Major Rockford?"

"Well, I guess he and the colonel know about it, but they won't interfere unless it gets too strenuous."

Dick and Paul found a large crowd of the older cadets already gathered in the gymnasium. In one corner was huddled a rather frightened group of freshmen, who were waiting their turn to be grilled. They had been rounded up from their rooms by a committee appointed for that purpose.

"Now, fellows," said Dutton, who, as usual, assumed the leadership, "we'll work 'em off in bunches. Put two or three of 'em in a blanket and toss 'em up for a starter."

"Some of 'em may get hurt," objected Stiver. "We'd better take 'em one at a time."

"Aw, you're afraid! Besides, we haven't time. Here, Beeby, grab a couple of 'em and pass 'em over."

Captain Beeby of Company B grasped a cadet in either hand, and shoved them toward Dutton. The latter already had one, and the three lads were pushed down into a large blanket which had been spread for that purpose.

"Grab the corners and up with 'em!" called Dutton. "Toss 'em as high as you can."

"Suppose they fall out?" objected Lieutenant Jim Watkins.

"It won't matter. There's a gym. mat under 'em."

Up into the air went the unfortunate lads, clinging together in a sort of bunch, and struggling to see which one was to be underneath in the fall. Down they came into the blanket, but the impact was so heavy that it was torn from the grasp of the cadets holding it, and the freshmen landed on the mat with a thump and many squeals.

"That's the way!" cried Dutton with a laugh. "Now, once more."

"Let's take some others," proposed Beeby.

"No, they haven't had enough."

So, in spite of their struggles and protests, the lads were tossed again. Then three more took their places. They, too, had a hard time, one falling over the edge of the blanket and partly off the mat. But he was game and never made a sound.

"Now for the slide of death!" cried Dutton.

"What's that?" asked several of his cronies.

"I'll show you," he said.

From the top of the gymnasium there hung a long rope, running over a pulley. Dutton made a loop in one end, and then took hold of the other.

"Tie a couple of 'em up in blankets," he ordered, and two of the struggling cadets were made up into a rough bundle. Dutton then passed several coils of the long rope about them.

"Pull 'em up!" he ordered next, and willing hands aided him in hoisting the lads toward the roof of the gymnasium.

"You are now about to take the slide of death!" called Dutton, when the freshmen were close against the pulley, and fully forty feet above the floor. "We're going to let you come down on the run——"

A scream from one of the lads in the blanket high up in the air interrupted him.

"You'll frighten him!" called Dick.

"What's that to you? Mind your own affairs, and we'll run this," said Dutton. "Or maybe you'll get your hazing, which we omitted last time."

"Go ahead," said Dick. "But that's too risky."

"Aw, cut it out, Hamilton," said Stiver. "We ain't going to hurt 'em."

But this assurance could not be heard by the lads in the blanket, who could not see.

"Let her slide!" cried Dutton, and he and his chums released their grasp on the rope, which was wound about a post.

Down, on the run, came the unfortunate cadets, and from the cries they uttered they must have imagined that they were about to be dashed to the floor. Then Dick saw that several mats were right under them, in case of accident.

But it was not the intention of Dutton to run any risks. At first the rope was paid out swiftly, and then it was gradually tightened against the post, until the speed of the falling cadets was slackened, and they came to a stop a few inches above the mats.

"The next batch won't get off so lucky!" announced Dutton, as he commanded that some more be wrapped up in the blanket. "We'll bump them."

This news was sufficient to cause a panic among the candidates still remaining, but their protests were of no avail, and they came down with considerable force on the mats, but no one was hurt.

Then the water cure was administered to a number, the streams being poured down their trouser legs, amid the laughter of the unfortunate ones who were exempt. As the gymnasium was kept quite warm this ordeal was not so bad as might be supposed. Still, it was not pleasant, but it was part of the game.

A particularly tall freshman was stretched out, or, rather suspended on the flying rings, until he looked like some soaring eagle. He struggled, but to no effect, and had to take his medicine. Others were blindfolded, and made to fight with blown-up bladders, some were tied in pairs on trapezes, and a number were made to do ridiculous stunts, to the more or less enjoyment of the older cadets.

"Well, I guess that's all," announced Dutton, a little before it was time for taps to sound. "Unless we take Hamilton."

"I'm willing," said Dick, with a grim smile.

"He's too willing. He'd knock a lot of us around," whispered Stiver to Dutton.

"We'll postpone your initiation," remarked the Captain of Company A. "Come on, fellows, there goes tattoo. Half an hour to lights out."

Matters more quickly adjusted themselves following the opening of the winter term, than they did at the beginning of the fall one, as there were fewer new cadets. Lessons were quickly under way, together with a few drills, out of doors when the weather permitted it, otherwise in the big hall.

The lake froze over, and Dick and the other lads had their fill of skating, races being held every afternoon. In a number of these, particularly the long distance ones, Dick came in a winner.

Then there were snowball fights between the different companies, both on foot and mounted on horses, with wooden shields. These were lively affairs, and were enjoyed by all.

Dick took his part in the winter sports, but, though he had increased his friends by the addition of several freshmen, particularly Payson Emery, the lad whose knocking down by Dutton he had resented, he made no progress toward getting intimate with the upperclassmen.

"But I've got half a term yet," thought Dick.

With the advent of winter, affairs in the town of Kentfield, which was about two miles from where the academy was located, became more lively. There were theatrical and other entertainments, and the cadets, when they could not get permission to attend these, used to run the guard.

Usually there was little risk in this, as the cadet officers would not report their friends, unless some member of the academy faculty happened to hear a late-staying party come sneaking in, and then the young officer on guard knew he had to make some sort of a report or be punished himself.

One night there was a large and rather fashionable dance given in town, by some friends of Dutton's family. He was invited, together with some of his cronies, but he was refused permission to go, as he had broken several rules of late.

"Well, I'm going anyhow," he announced to Stiver. "I guess I can run the guard all right, and get back. There are some girls I want to meet."

So Dutton and Stiver, and one or two others, went.

Dick was on guard, as it happened, at the barracks where Dutton and the others had their rooms. He was patrolling his post long after midnight, expecting soon to be relieved, when he saw some shadowy forms stealing along the hedge.

"Halt!" he cried, bringing his rifle up.

"Gee! It's Hamilton!" he heard some one say, and he recognized Stiver's voice.

"Then I guess it's all up with us," announced Dutton, straightening up, and, with his chums, approaching Dick.

The young millionaire said nothing.

"Are you going to let us in? We haven't the countersign," said Dutton, with an uneasy laugh.

"You can go in," replied Dick, producing the key to the front door.

"And I suppose you'll squeal in the morning," went on Dutton, as he and his cronies entered.

Dick didn't answer.

"You should have known better than to risk going, Dutton," said Stiver. "Of course he'll tell. He owes you too much not to."

But Dick didn't tell, and Dutton's breach of discipline was not discovered.

CHAPTER XXI

THE FANCY DRESS BALL

"Well, Dick," remarked Paul Drew, one afternoon, as he and his roommate came in from drill, "I see you're on the ball committee."

"What ball, and what committee?"

"The fancy dress ball, if I have to go into all the details. You know the academy has one every year, and it's a swell affair, let me tell you. Lights, gay music, pretty girls——"

"Especially pretty girls," said Dick with a smile. "But what committee am I on?"

"Arrangements. Didn't you see the list posted in the mess hall? I don't envy you. There will be lots to do."

"Suppose you take pity on my ignorance, and go a little more into details."

Whereupon Paul did, describing the affair at length. It was to take place, as usual, in February, and this time would be held on Washington's birthday.

"Maybe we won't have fun!" exclaimed Paul. "There'll be all sorts of costumes, and the decorations will be immense. You'll have to help with them."

"Then I'd better get busy," declared Dick. "I must see who's chairman of my committee, and report for work. What character are you going to portray, Paul?"

"I think I shall go as a Colonial officer. I always did like a powdered wig."

"Talcum powder, instead of gun powder," retorted Dick. "That's the calibre of such tin soldiers as you."

"Halt!" called Paul, as Dick prepared to run away. "As punishment I'll not introduce you to a certain pretty girl I know, who is coming to the dance."

"Then I'll surrender and beg your pardon!" cried Dick.

"What part will you play?" asked Paul. "You'd look swell dressed as an Indian."

"I think I'll take the part of a cannon swab, and then I'll not have to bother about a suit. But more of that later. I'm going to see what I have to do."

Dick found out from the chairman of his committee that there was plenty of work to prepare for the fête, and he did his share. One day he had to go to a nearby town to purchase some of the decorations.

It was two days before the fancy dress ball was to take place, and, having made his purchases, Dick prepared to return to the Academy. As he was about to board a trolley car, which ran near Kentfield, he heard a voice calling:

"How are you, Dick Hamilton?"

He turned, to see a tall, well-built lad, of about his own age, who was smiling at him in a friendly fashion. At first he did not recognize the youth.

"You don't know me, I see," went on the other. "I once had the pleasure of interviewing you about a gold brick game——"

"Why, Larry Dexter! How are you?" cried Dick, turning aside from the car, and holding out his hand to the other. "I did not get a good look at you, or I would have known you at once. What good wind blows you here? Can't you stay and come over to our Academy? Where have you been? How is the newspaper business?"

"My, you'd do for a reporter yourself!" exclaimed Larry Dexter, with a smile. "I'm glad you haven't forgotten me though. Have you been swindled lately? I'd like a good story. The one I came down here after didn't pan out."

Those of you who have read my books in the "Newspaper Series" will at once recognize the lad who greeted Dick. He was Lawrence Dexter, a reporter on the New York *Leader*, and, as related in the volume called "Dick Hamilton's Fortune," he had met our hero when the latter had narrowly escaped being swindled by a sharper in the metropolis. Larry, as all his friends called him, had managed to get a good "story" from the experience of Dick, who was on a visit to New York, with a number of boy friends. The incident is mentioned in the third volume of the Newspaper Series, "Larry Dexter's Great Search," where the young reporter does some detective work.

After Dick had given Larry the story of the attempted swindle, the young reporter took the millionaire's son to the newspaper office, and showed him something of how a great daily is published. The two lads had struck up quite a friendship, and they had pleasant memories of each other.

"What are you doing here?" asked Dick, as they walked up the street with his newspaper acquaintance.

"Oh, I came here on a peculiar robbery yarn, but it turned out to be an ordinary affair, and not worth much of a story. I sent in the account by wire, and, as a reward for my past valuable services to the paper, I have been given a couple of days' leave of absence. You see, the managing editor thinks quite highly of me," and Larry made a mock bow.

"Then you're just in time," said Dick.

"How so?"

"Why, you can spend a few days with me. There's going to be a big masked ball at the military academy where I attend, and perhaps you'd like to see it."

"I think I would, if the military authorities will admit a mere civilian."

"I'm sure they will. Come along back with me. I'll introduce you to Colonel Masterly, and you can bunk in with Drew and me. Paul Drew is my roommate—a fine fellow."

"Oh, I'm afraid I'll put you out."

"You couldn't do that, Larry. Come on. We'll have some fun."

So Larry Dexter accompanied Dick back to the Academy, where he was speedily made welcome by Colonel Masterly and members of the latter's staff.

"We would be very glad to have you remain and witness some evolutions of the cadets, a day or so after the ball," invited the colonel. "They will possibly interest you."

"I should be glad to," replied Larry, "but I can't stay long enough. It is very kind of you to invite me to the ball."

Possibly Colonel Masterly had a purpose in seconding Dick's invitation to this affair. The head of the military school was not averse to a little free advertising for the Academy, and he thought perhaps Larry might "write up" an account of the ball. Which, as a matter of fact, Larry did, and a fine account it was.

The reporter, though Dick invited him to don a costume, thought it better not to, and, when the night of the gay affair came, Larry was in sober black, forming a strange contrast to the lads in gay uniforms. The dresses of the young ladies and the uniforms or costumes of the cadets, with the hundreds of electric lights, the gay streamers and flags festooned about the gymnasium, made the apartment a brilliant picture. The Academy cadet band struck up a lively march, and the dancers paraded around the room, two by two. Dick was not in this, as he had not yet made the acquaintance of any of the girls, and after ascertaining that Larry Dexter was in a position where he could see well, our hero retired rather disconsolately to a secluded corner. He saw Paul Drew dancing with a very pretty girl, and was just beginning to envy him, when his roommate walked up, and introduced her to Dick.

"Allow me to present my friend, Dick Hamilton," said Paul with a low bow. "Mr. Hamilton—Miss Fordice. Dick is a better dancer than I am," added Paul.

It was plainly a hint to Dick, who at once took advantage of it, and asked:

"May I have the honor?"

"If it pleases you, sir," replied the girl, with a mischievous smile, and an old-fashioned courtesy.

Dick led her into a two-step, and they were soon whirling about. But Dick was not selfish, and he knew better than to keep Paul's partner away from him for long, so, making some excuse, he led Miss Fordice back to his roommate.

"I'll introduce you to some other girls, after this dance, Hamilton," Paul called back to him.

Dick noticed that a tall, dark girl, who was standing near one of the pillars, started at the sound of his name. A moment later she advanced toward him, appeared to hesitate, and then came forward.

"Excuse me," she said, "but are you Dick Hamilton?"

"I am," said our hero, secretly delighted at the chance of talking to the girl.

"I thought I heard Mr. Drew call you that. You must think it dreadfully forward of me to speak to you without an introduction——"

"Nothing of the sort," said Dick promptly.

"But I know friends of yours," went on the girl. "I am Miss Mabel Hanford, and I know Birdy Lee, who lives in your town—I mean in the place where you come from. She and I used to be great chums. We went to school together."

"Indeed," said Dick. "Birdy Lee and I are well acquainted."

"So she said when I wrote to her, telling her I was coming to this ball. She suggested that I might meet you, and when I heard your name mentioned, I couldn't help speaking."

"I am glad you did," said Dick, smiling.

"Won't you come over and let me introduce you to my mother?" went on Miss Hanford. "I feel as if I had known you a long time, for Birdy often spoke of you in her letters to me."

"I am glad she did," said Dick, gallantly.

Mrs. Hanford greeted him kindly, evidently approving of her daughter's action.

"May I have the next dance?" asked Dick of the daughter.

"Yes," said Miss Hanford, blushing a little. "But I hope you don't think I spoke to you just to have you dance with me——"

"Not at all," Dick hastened to say.

"Because my card is nearly filled now," she went on.

"I hope I may find room to put my name down in several places."

"You may look. I think the next waltz is open."

"It seems to be the only one," said Dick, ruefully.

A little later he and the girl were sailing about the room to the strains of a dreamy waltz. Dick was a fine dancer, Miss Hanford was his equal, and the two made a pleasing appearance on the big ballroom floor.

"Where were you?" asked Paul, as Dick came walking up to him after the young millionaire had taken his partner back to her mother. "I was looking for you to introduce a girl to you."

"I managed to meet one myself."

"Who?"

"Miss Mabel Hanford."

Paul whistled.

"What's the matter?" asked Dick. "Isn't she all right?"

"I should say so! Every fellow here is anxious to dance with her, but Dutton seems to monopolize her. He seems to think he's engaged to her."

"I don't believe he has any right to think that," spoke Dick warmly. "She's a very nice girl. I wish I had met her earlier in the evening." The band was playing another waltz.

"So do lots of other fellows, I guess. But you're doing pretty well. There goes Dutton with her now," continued Paul.

Dick looked on, with envious eyes. Though Dutton and Miss Hanford were waltzing about, she did not seem at ease. Her face was flushed, and Dutton looked angry. When the dance came to an end he left her abruptly.

Dick strolled over, casually, though his heart was beating faster than usual.

"You look warm," he said to the girl.

"Yes, the room is very close," she replied, and she fanned her face with a filmy lace handkerchief.

"Perhaps you would like an ice."

"Indeed I should."

"I'll get you one," promised Dick. Then, waxing bold, he looked at her program.

"What are you looking for?" she asked with a laugh. "To see what sort of ice I prefer? It's not there, but I'll take orange, if you can get one."

"I was looking to see, if by any good fortune you had another vacant place on your card."

"I'll make one for you," she said with a smile, as she crossed out a name. "Tantrell can look for another partner," she added.

"Who may Tantrell be?" asked Dick, as he put his name in place of the erased one.

"My cousin. He brought me here, but he doesn't care much for dancing. I know he'll be glad to have you relieve him."

"Not half so glad as I am," retorted Dick quickly. "Now I'll get you the ice."

As he walked away he saw Dutton eyeing him angrily.

"Probably he doesn't like me to be talking to her," thought Dick.

There was quite a crush in the refreshment room, and, in spite of the fact that he was a member of the arrangement committee, Dick had some difficulty in getting an ice for Miss Hanford. As he struggled through the crush of gay dancers with it he tripped, and, to save himself, involuntarily threw his hands forward. The ice slipped from the plate, and went splashing full against the back of a cadet dressed in an elaborate Colonial uniform, with a white satin coat. The highly-colored ice made a big, blotchy stain on the garment.

The cadet whirled like a flash. It was Dutton.

"Who did that?" he cried, as he saw a little puddle forming at his feet, where the fast melting ice lay.

"I did," answered Dick promptly. "It was an accident, Captain Dutton."

"An accident?" There was a sneer in the other's tone.

"An accident," retorted Dick, as he turned away.

"Here! Where are you going?" cried Dutton. Several turned to stare at him, for his manner toward Dick was most insulting.

"I am going after another ice for Miss Hanford," said the young millionaire quickly.

"Wait a minute!" ordered Dutton, in the voice he used on parade.

"Not now," drawled Dick. "Wait until I get another ice."

"You wait, I say!" spluttered Dutton.

"It's too hot," replied Dick, for he could not help but notice the insulting tones. "I'll see you later. I'm sorry about the accident."

"That was no accident," declared Dutton. "You did that on purpose, and I—I want——"

But Dick passed on. He saw Miss Hanford looking at him from among the fringe of spectators, and, as he walked back to the refreshment room, he noticed that Dutton had one of the mess-hall attendants wiping off as much as possible of the stain from the white satin coat.

CHAPTER XXII

THE CHALLENGE

When Dick secured another ice, and took it to Miss Hanford, he found her sitting in a quiet corner. She was rather pale, and did not seem to care much for the ice which he had had such trouble in securing.

"I'm not quite so warm now," she said, in explanation. "It was very kind of you to get this for me. Do you—do you think Captain Dutton will be very angry at you?" She seemed anxious.

"I don't see why he should be," replied Dick. "It was an accident. I could not help tripping."

"After you went back the second time, he talked loudly about you having done it on purpose, and he said he was going to demand satisfaction," went on the girl. "Will he?"

"Well, he can demand it, I suppose," said Dick slowly, "but I don't know what I can do, except to say I'm sorry, and offer to pay for his coat."

"Do you—do you think he will do anything—anything desperate?" asked Miss Hanford, and she looked at Dick sharply.

"Of course not," he replied. "But if we are going to dance, would you mind if we began now? I think this is my two-step."

She arose, and they went whirling about the room. But she was strangely quiet. Dick's enjoyment of the dance was not a bit lessened by seeing Dutton once more scowling at him from behind a draped pillar. The cadet captain had doffed his gay coat, and wore one belonging to his uniform. It formed a strange contrast to his otherwise Colonial costume. When the dance was over Dick saw him beckoning, and, excusing himself from his fair partner, he walked to where Dutton stood.

"You wished to speak to me?" asked Dick.

"Yes. Come outside."

"What for?"

"I wish to speak to you."

"Won't it do in here?"

"No!" snapped Dutton.

Dick hesitated a moment, and, not wishing to quarrel with the captain in the ballroom, he followed him out on a verandah.

"What do you mean by insulting me, and making me ridiculous?" demanded Dutton fiercely.

"Insulting you?" repeated Dick.

"That's what I said. You refused to come back when I called you. I'm your superior officer."

"Not on an occasion like this!" exclaimed Dick, and he drew himself up, and looked Dutton straight in the eyes. "We are all equal here to-night, Captain Dutton. I take no orders from you!"

"We'll see about that. Why did you deliberately spill that ice over me? You wanted to make me the laughing stock of everyone in the room!"

"I did not. You have no right to say that. It was an accident, pure and simple, and I have already apologized to you for it."

"That is not enough. No one can insult me with impunity. I demand satisfaction!"

"I don't see what satisfaction I can give you—unless I buy you a new coat. If that is what you what you want I will be happy to send you a check for whatever amount——"

"Hold on, Hamilton!" cried Dutton hoarsely. "This is going too far! You're getting mighty fresh. I suppose because you are a millionaire you think your money will do anything. But I tell you it won't. You can't buy a gentleman with money, nor make one either. You come here with a lot of millions behind you, and you think all you need to do is to insult a gentleman, and then offer to pay for it. I tell you I'll not stand it. You did that on purpose and——"

"I have already told you that I did not."

"And I say you did."

There was no mistaking Dutton's meaning. Dick took a step forward. His face was slightly pale.

"That will do!" he said sternly. "Are you aware that you have practically accused me of telling an untruth?"

"That's what I meant to do," answered Dutton fiercely. "You're a cad—a sneak—you threw that ice at me on purpose!"

"If you say that again," exclaimed Dick, "I'll——"

"Well, what will you do?" sneered Dutton.

"I think I shall have to buy you two coats," spoke Dick calmly, for he saw that Dutton was losing control of his temper, and the young millionaire wanted to end the affair.

"Don't you give me any of your fresh talk!" cried the captain.

"I shall say what I please on an occasion like this," responded Dick. "I have that privilege."

"You have, eh? Then look out for yourself!"

Dutton fairly leaped forward, and endeavored to strike Dick, but the young millionaire was too quick for him, and stepped to one side, at the same time involuntarily shooting out his fist, which caught the bully in the side. Dutton stopped short.

"I suppose you know what striking a gentleman means," he said slowly.

"I do when I hit one. I haven't struck any gentleman to-night," said Dick coolly.

"You're adding insult to it. You've got to give me satisfaction for this!"

"I suppose so. You recall how it turned out last time."

"This time will be different. You won't get off so easily."

"Have your own way about it. I guess Paul Drew will be my second again, but I should think you'd had enough of fighting."

"Not with you! I'll never be satisfied until I've beaten you!"

"Then you'll wait a long time."

The two had talked in rather low but tense tones, and they were not aware that they were directly beneath a window that had been opened to let in the fresh air. Nor did they see the frightened face of a girl at the casement.

"Will after the ball suit you?" asked Dutton, as he turned aside.

"Any time."

Dick remained in the cool winter air a little longer, filling his lungs with the oxygen, and when he returned to the ballroom he saw no sign of Dutton. Nor did he see Miss Hanford, though he looked for her, as he had another dance coming.

Supper was served soon after this, and Dick had no sooner risen from the table than Paul Drew signalled him to step one side.

"Dutton has sent a challenge to you by Stiver," he said.

"I expected it."

"Yes, but what do you think he wants?"

"What?"

"To fight with swords."

"Swords?"

"Yes. Like the students do in German schools. Heads and body protected so you can't either be more than scratched. I think it's silly, but of course I said I'd tell you."

"That's right. Swords, eh? Well, with football helmets on, and a baseball chest protector, and heavy gloves, I guess it won't be dangerous. But what's the use of fighting if some one doesn't get hurt? I prefer my fists."

"Dutton's idea seems to be for you both to be rigged out as we are when we practice with broadswords on horses," said Paul, referring to one of the drills taught at the school.

"Well, I don't like to object," said Dick, "but it strikes me that as the challenged party, I have the choice of weapons."

"So you have. I forgot that. Then you don't want swords?"

"I'll tell you later. You can inform Dutton I'll fight him when and where he pleases, and that, as it's my right, I'll name the weapons when we meet."

"All right. Give him a good lesson, Dick."

Paul went off to carry the message, and Dick, seeing Miss Hanford, went up to her for the waltz. She gave him a place made vacant by the inability of her partner to claim her, as he was on the supper committee. Dick thought the girl seemed nervous and alarmed, but he did not speak of it.

The dance lasted until two o'clock in the morning, and then the guests began leaving. Dick was somewhat surprised to see Miss Hanford in apparently earnest conversation with grizzled Major Webster, but he concluded that she was only telling him what a good time she had had.

"Won't you call and see me sometime?" she asked Dick, as she bade him good-night.

"I will be pleased to," he said.

"And don't—don't have any quarrel with Captain Dutton," she said, with a little smile.

"Er—oh, no, I—I—er—I won't," was all Dick could stammer. He resolved that he would have no more quarrels, but it was too late to stop this one.

As the last of the guests were leaving, Paul sought out his roommate.

"The clump of trees, down by the lagoon," he whispered. "In an hour. What about weapons? Dutton wants to know."

"He'll have to wait. I'll bring them with me. It's my privilege."

A little later Dick went to his room, where he was busy for some time. When he emerged he was accompanied by Paul. He wore his long cape overcoat, and something bulged beneath it.

"I guess he'll be surprised," commented Paul.

The clump of trees, which Dutton had selected as the place for the duel, was located on a little point of land that jutted out into the lake, and near a small lagoon. It was some distance from the academy buildings, and out of sight. The trees had kept most of the snow from the ground, and it was a sheltered place. As there was a full moon there was no need of other light.

As Dick and Paul approached the place they saw several dark figures moving about.

"They're on time," whispered Paul.

"Yes. I hope the Colonel doesn't hear of it."

As they drew nearer, Stiver stepped forward and said:

"Is your man ready, Drew?"

"All ready."

"Then we demand to know the weapons. My principal will object to pistols, as they make too much noise."

"My principal has the choice of weapons, as you know, and unless he is allowed to exercise it we must decline to fight."

Paul spoke as though it was very serious.

"I know, but, hang it all, man, we can't fight with pistols. We'd have the whole crowd down on us," objected Stiver, in some alarm.

"I'll not fight with pistols," put in Dutton, which was a wrong thing for a brave duelist to do.

"Don't be worried," replied Dick coolly. "I have not selected pistols. But we are delaying too long. I am ready."

"So are we," said Stiver, but it was observed that his voice was not very steady. He was beginning to wish he had had nothing to do with this. It seemed to be getting serious, and he, as well as Dutton, wondered what Dick could be carrying under his overcoat.

"Take your places," said Paul.

"But the weapons," insisted Stiver.

"My principal will hand one to your principal as soon as he takes his place," went on Paul. "We seconds must retire to a safe distance."

"They—they aren't rifles, are they?" asked Stiver, and this time his voice was very shaky.

"They are not rifles," said Dick, somewhat solemnly. "Come, I can't stay here all night. I want to write an account of this to Miss Hanford."

"Don't you dare!" cried Dutton.

"Hush! Take your place," said his second.

Dutton approached Dick, and held out his hand to receive his weapon. Dick unfolded his coat and extended—not a sword or gun, but a big bladder, fully blown up, and tied to a short stick. He kept a similar one for himself.

"These are my weapons," he said.

"I won't fight with those! It's an insult! I demand satisfaction!" fairly shouted Dutton.

"Hush!" cried Stiver. "Someone is coming!"

But it was too late. Several figures could be seen running over the snow toward the duelists.

CHAPTER XXIII

A WINTER MARCH

"Quick! Here comes Major Webster!" cried Stiver. There was no mistaking the soldierly figure who was approaching.

"And Colonel Masterly is with him!" added Paul.

"Some one has squealed!" added Dutton, but he seemed rather glad than otherwise that the duel had been interrupted.

"Cut for it!" said Dick. "Across the ice, and into the grove! We can get in the back way, and they won't know who it was out here."

"Say, if they were tipped off that something like this was going to take place, they know who was in it," said Paul, as he and Dick headed across the ice which covered the inlet at one side of the wooded point.

Dick thought of the conversation he had seen taking place between Miss Hanford and the major, and a light came to him.

"She must have overheard the talk about swords, and she got frightened," he said to himself. "That's how the major knew."

On came the dark figures over the snow, but the cadets had a good start. Across the ice they went, and were soon lost in the depths of a little grove of trees. From there they managed to gain the barracks.

"Queer they didn't call after us," said Dick, as he and Paul were safe in their room.

"That is sort of funny. Say, where's the other bladder?"

"Dutton must have it."

But Dutton didn't have it. He had dropped it as he ran, and Major Webster picked it up a little later on the dueling ground. The major held it out to Colonel Masterly.

"What's this?" asked the colonel.

"One of their weapons, I fancy."

"Then it was all a joke. What Miss Hanford told you about the duel, she must have dreamed."

"No, she says she overheard Dutton challenge Hamilton, and later on, some talk between Hamilton and Drew. She was very much frightened, and came and told me. Of course I know the cadets will fight once in a while. They wouldn't be any good if they didn't, and, though you and I know that it's against the rules, it's no more than you and I used to do. But when she spoke of swords I thought it time to take a hand."

"But they didn't have swords."

"Evidently not. Hamilton reserved to himself the choice of weapons, as the challenged party, she said, and it seems that he selected bladders."

"But why?"

"I fancy he wanted to teach Dutton a lesson. There is bad blood between them, I have heard in roundabout ways, and once Hamilton administered a good drubbing to Dutton."

"Hum! Well, I don't see that there is anything for us to do."

"No, only go to bed. I'm sleepy. The time was when I could stay up at a ball all night, and attend a duel at sunrise, but those days are past. I think we'd better say nothing about this."

"Just as you like, major. You are in charge of the cadets. But perhaps we had better let Miss Hanford know that there was no bloody conflict."

"I will. Poor little girl! She was quite worried."

So that was how the duel between Dick and Dutton turned out. It did not add to the good feeling between the two cadets. Dick would have been glad to be on friendly terms, but Dutton considered that he had been made the butt of a joke, and he hated Dick more than ever. He threatened to get even until Dick sent word to him that if he liked he would meet him with bare fists as weapons, and have the matter out. Dutton knew better than to agree to this.

Of course Larry Dexter heard about the duel, but at Dick's request the young reporter sent no account of it to his paper, which described the fancy dress ball at some length. Larry remained Dick's guest three days, and greatly enjoyed his visit to the academy.

In order to give the cadets a taste of as many varieties of military life as possible, and to show them that they could not always expect summer weather and sunny skies, Major Webster decided to have a winter practice march.

This was announced for a date late in January, and some novel features were to be incorporated. The cadets were to be divided into several small squads, and were to set off at different times from the academy, to reach a certain point ten miles distant, report there for dinner, and march back. Various routes were selected, with officers stationed at checking points, and the squad which made the best time was to receive a trophy.

As the ground was quite thickly covered with snow, and as certain landmarks, plainly visible in summer, were now obliterated, the march would prove no easy one. It was to be made on horses, and only the best riders were allowed to participate.

"That's the kind of a stunt I like," said Dick, the morning of the proposed winter march. "We'll have some fun to-day, Paul, old boy."

"Yes, if we don't get caught in a blizzard. It looks like snow."

"So much the better. That will make it all the harder. I wish I was going to lead a squad."

"I don't. Who is in charge of ours?"

"Allen Rutledge. He's a good rider. Well, it's almost time to start. Whew! But it's cold!"

Dick's squad, in charge of Captain Rutledge of the football team, was the third to start off. They set their horses into a gentle canter, as they knew they would need all the strength of the animals ere the day was over.

At first it was pleasant enough, moving along over the snow, but, as it grew colder, it was not quite so much fun. Still the lads did not complain, as they knew the training was good for them.

When they had gone about five miles some flakes of snow sifted lazily down from the gray, leaden clouds overhead.

"I guess we're going to be in for it before we get back," observed Captain Rutledge. "Close up the ranks, behind there. Don't straggle."

They kept to their route, were checked at the proper point by an officer, and then started for the turning station. This was a hotel in a small town ten miles from the academy, and glad enough the cadets were to reach it, and find a hot dinner waiting for them.

An hour was allowed for luncheon, and the feeding of the horses, and then the start back was made. This was the most difficult part of the march, as the way led through an uninhabited part of the country, at the edge of the mountain range, and the roads were seldom traveled, and not of the best.

About three miles from where they had dinner was another checking station. Dick's squad reached this in the midst of quite a snowstorm.

"I guess it will only be a squall," observed Rutledge, as he went in the house, where the checking officer was stationed, to report.

"A squall?" observed Dick. "If this doesn't keep up until we get back, and for some time after, I'm a Dutchman."

Rutledge came out of the house, followed by the checking officer, Captain Nelton. Both looked worried.

"We'll keep watch for them," said Rutledge as he prepared to vault into the saddle.

"Yes, I wish you would," said Captain Nelton. "They may have straggled behind, and lost the road. Have them join your squad if you see them."

"What's up?" asked Dick, for an air of familiar fellowship was permitted on the practice marches.

"Dutton and Stiver didn't report in with their squad, which is just ahead of ours," replied Rutledge. "We're to look out for them."

"Most likely they sneaked off to have a good time somewhere," said Dick in a low voice to Paul.

The pace was slower now, for the snow was deeper, and the horses were beginning to feel the strain of the long march. The flakes were falling thicker and faster, and from the rear the leader of the squad could not be seen.

"Come, boys, close ranks!" called Rutledge several times. "If you stray off now you'll be in danger. Keep together."

They tried to, but some horses went better than others, and it was impossible for the stragglers to keep up with the leaders at all times. Rutledge saw this and called to Dick:

"Here, Hamilton, you and Drew are good riders. You take the rear, and keep it as close to me as you can. This storm is getting fierce."

It was almost a blizzard now, with the wind sobbing and moaning in the trees, and the white flakes cutting into one's face with stinging force.

"Take the next turn to the right," called Rutledge to Dick and Paul, as they wheeled their horses and started for the rear.

They heard faintly through the noise of the storm, and answered back. They succeeded for a time in keeping the end riders up toward the front, urging their somewhat jaded horses to a trot. Then, all at once, they found themselves out of sight of the tails of the end animals.

"Hit is up a little," suggested Dick to Paul. "They're leaving us."

They spurred their horses ahead, but they never noticed as they bent their heads to avoid the blast that they kept straight on, instead of taking the turn to the right, where the road divided. So fast was the snow falling, drifting as it did so, that the tracks of the horses just ahead of them were almost blotted out.

"They must be galloping," said Dick. "Come on, Paul."

They urged their wearied horses to a gallop, expecting soon to come within sight of the rear of the squad. But, as they went on and on, the road became more impassable. The snow was at least two feet deep now, and more was falling every minute.

"I can't see anything of them," said Paul, peering ahead into the white mist.

"Me either. Let's give a yell."

They called, but the echo was their only reply.

"Can you see any tracks?" asked Dick, leaning over in the saddle, and scanning the ground.

"No. Can you?"

"Not a one."

The lads straightened up, and looked at each other. Their steeds whinnied helplessly, complaining thus of the cold.

"Dick," said Paul, "I believe we've taken the wrong turn."

"I didn't see any turn to take. We've come a straight road."

"I don't believe so. Rutledge said something about turning to the right."

"I know he did, but I didn't see any turn."

"Neither did I, but we're certainly on the wrong road now. This hasn't been traveled this winter."

"Looks that way. Say, we've come up the side of the mountain. I wondered what made the horses so blown."

It needed but a glance to show that this was so. Unconsciously they had taken a path leading up the mountain, and they were now on what was evidently a wood-road, in the midst of a forest.

As they stood there, vainly starting about, there came a fiercer burst of the storm, and on the wings of a stinging, cold wind there came such a cloud of snow flakes that they could not see ten feet ahead of them.

"We're caught in a blizzard!" shouted Dick. "We must keep close together, Paul."

CHAPTER XXIV

THE RESCUE OF DUTTON

Through the blinding snow the two cadets tried to peer, in order to see which way they should take to get back to the academy. Neither of them was very familiar with the country, though they had been over part of it in drills and practice marches in the fall. But things wore a different aspect now.

"Which way had we better go?" asked Paul, after a pause. He had to shout to be heard above the noise of the gale.

"I guess the best plan is to keep down the mountain," replied Dick. "We'll strike a road sooner or later leading to Kentfield."

The horses did not like to face the blast, but the young cadets forced them about, and the unwilling steeds started down the slope.

Protected though they were by their heavy winter clothing and overcoats, the two lads felt the cold bitterly. But they were too plucky to give up. The horses could not be urged to more than a walk, and, indeed, faster pace was not safe, as they did not know what the snow might conceal.

As they went down the mountain side they kept a watch for the sight of any objects that would indicate a road, or tell them their whereabouts. But all they could see was an expanse of snow, a whirling, white cloud of flakes, with here and there the black trunks of trees standing up like grim sentinels.

"We might as well be a thousand miles from nowhere," called Dick.

"That's right," answered his companion. "I wonder if we're going straight?"

"Isn't much choice. We'll be on level ground in a little while, anyhow. Then the going will be better."

They emerged from the thickly wooded side of the big hill, and came upon a plain, which did not look familiar. It was open country, however, and this was better than being in the woods, though the cold wind had more of a sweep over it.

"Now, which way?" asked Paul. "I've lost all sense of direction."

"And I'm not much better. Suppose we let the horses go as they please? Maybe they'll have sense enough to head toward their stables."

"Good idea, we'll do it."

They let the reins hang loose on the necks of the animals. The steeds hesitated for a moment, sniffed the air, and then started off to the left.

"I hope that's right, but it doesn't seem so," said Dick ruefully. "However, anything's better than standing still in this storm."

There was no let-up to the blizzard, which fairly enveloped the lads in its icy grasp.

They had traveled for perhaps a mile when Dick, who was a little in the lead, suddenly cried out:

"Hi, Paul! Here's a house, anyhow!"

"A house?"

"Yes. Straight ahead."

Paul looked through the whirling clouds of snow, and saw something dark looming up about thirty yards away.

"Maybe it's a barn," he said.

"Even that's all right; but where there's a barn there's most likely to be a house. I guess we're all right now."

Their horses stumbled on, over the uneven ground, and soon another big object loomed up through the snow.

"There's the house!" cried Dick. "Come on."

They managed to urge their horses to a trot, and, a few moments later, were knocking at the door of a large, white farmhouse. A pretty girl who opened it exclaimed:

"Come right in. I expect you're most frozen, aren't you?"

"Pretty nearly," replied Dick, as he entered with Paul.

They were soon near a warm fire, partaking of hot tea, though they declined the offer of some hard cider, an invitation slyly given by the farmer, who introduced himself as Enos Weatherby. His place was about eight miles from Kentfield, and, in the course of his talk, Dick and Paul learned that Captain Dutton and Lieutenant Stiver had been at the house a little while before, and had not refused the cider.

This was news to Dick, but he at once saw how matters stood. Dutton and his companion, he learned, knew the two daughters of the farmer, and had called on them during the practice march. It was on this account that they had not reported at the checking point. Probably they thought they could make a circuit, visit their friends, and join their squad in time to report at the academy, trusting to luck to explain their temporary absence.

They had been gone about an hour, Mr. Weatherby said, and he showed Dick and Paul the road they had taken, a short cut to the school.

"Ride down this road," explained the farmer, "cut across my big meadow, and you will come to the main highway. Keep along that until you come to the first cross road, turn to the left and you'll get to the road that leads around the lake. Then it's only a mile to the school. But you're welcome to stay all night. The storm is getting worse."

"Thank you, very much," replied Dick, "but we couldn't stay. Colonel Masterly would be worried about us. We'll take the short cut home. I guess they'll call the march a dead heat as far as picking a winner is concerned."

The girls added their entreaties to those of their father and Mrs. Weatherby, who had been busy at household duties, entered the dining room, to urge the cadets to remain, as she had plenty of room. But Dick and Paul would not.

There was obvious disappointment in the good-byes of the two girls, but Dick and Paul cared little for that, though the two Miss Weatherbys were rather pretty, even if they were a bit silly.

The two wayfarers thanked their hosts, and, feeling much refreshed and warmed, while the horses, too, had improved by the halt, they set off again.

The snow was not coming down so fast, but it was much colder, and they hastened on, anxious to get to the academy.

"Queer about Dutton, wasn't it?" asked Dick.

"It sure was," agreed Paul. "He'll get into trouble if he doesn't look out."

"Somehow he always seems to escape, but I s'pose he'll do it once too often. This must be where we turn."

"I guess so. Go ahead."

They turned into the big meadow, crossed it, and came out into a road that showed some signs of travel. It was deserted now, however, as the winter night was settling down.

"A few more miles, and then for a good, hot supper," commented Dick "Don't talk about it," said Paul. "It makes me hungry."

Suddenly his horse shied, and the cadet, looking to see what caused it, beheld a dark object, half buried in the snow, at the side of the road.

"What's that?" called Dick, who had dropped a little to the rear.

"I don't know. Better take a look."

Dick forced his rather unwilling steed up to the object. The next moment he uttered a cry.

"It's a man!" he exclaimed.

He leaped off his horse, and bent closely to the black, huddled mass. Then he reached over and took hold of it.

"Here, Paul!" cried Dick. "Help me!"

"What is it?"

"It's Dutton, and he's unconscious and half frozen. Must have fallen from his horse and struck on his head! We must get him to shelter in a hurry."

Paul was quickly at his companion's side. He helped Dick lift the unconscious youth from the pile of snow. Dutton seemed to be trying to say something, but though his lips moved no sound came from them.

"What's the matter? Are you hurt?" asked Dick. "How did it happen?"

Dutton murmured something, but the words "horse" and "Stiver" were all they could distinguish.

"Maybe he's only fainted," suggested Paul. "Rub some snow on his face."

Dick tried this, but it was evident that Dutton was semi-conscious from the effects of some injury.

"What shall we do?" asked Paul, who was not used to acting in emergencies.

"We've got to get him to the academy as soon as possible."

"Maybe we had better take him back to the Weatherbys. That's nearer."

"Yes, but they wouldn't know how to take care of him. He needs a doctor. No, what we've got to do is to get him on my horse. He's stronger than yours, and can carry double. Then you ride on ahead and tell them to send a carriage."

Paul realized that this was the best thing to do, and the two, after some difficulty, hoisted Dutton to the back of Dick's steed. Then Dick mounted behind him, and, supporting in his arms the unconscious cadet, he set off through the snow. Paul galloped on ahead, urging his horse to a sharp gait, and made good time in reaching the academy.

There he found considerable confusion, and no little alarm, not only over the absence of Dutton, but over that of Dick and himself.

Paul quickly explained how he and his chum had become lost, and told how they had found Dutton. A carriage was at once sent out, and soon the injured lad was in the hospital, where anexamination showed that he was not badly hurt, having merely received a severe blow on the head.

"We feared something had happened when Dutton's horse came in without him," said Colonel Masterly. "Lieutenant Stiver said that he and Dutton became separated, after losing their way, and that he could not find him. So he came here to get help, and arrived just as Dutton's horse galloped in."

Dick told the colonel how he had found the young captain, but did not think it necessary to mention about the farmhouse and the two girls.

"I should have stopped the march when I saw that the weather was likely to be bad," the colonel said. "However, I am glad it is no worse."

Because of the incidents of the march it was called off, as far as a contest was concerned, and so no inquiry was made as to why Dutton and Stiver had failed to report at the checking point.

"I tell you what I think happened," said Paul, when he and Dick were discussing it in their room that night.

"Well, what?"

"I think Dutton and Stiver had more hard cider than was good for them. They must have quarreled, and Stiver left Dutton, who later fell from his horse. There was no excuse for them losing each other after they left Weatherby's house, and Dutton is too good a horseman to fall off, unless he couldn't take care of himself."

"Maybe you're right. I'm glad we found him, though."

"So am I, though I don't believe he'll treat you any better for saving his life."

"Oh, I don't know as I did that. Some one would have found him before he froze to death," said Dick.

Paul's idea of what had taken place between Dutton and Stiver seemed borne out by the coldness that sprang up between the two former cronies, as soon as Dutton could leave the hospital. He hardly spoke to the lieutenant of his company.

Nor was he specially cordial to our hero. In a stiff sort of fashion he thanked him for what he had done, but there was no semblance of real friendship, and Dutton's crowd did not take up with Dick, as they might, reasonably, have been expected to.

With the approach of spring the baseball fever began to stir in the veins of the cadets, and several nines were formed. Dick managed to get on a freshman team, much to his delight, for he was an excellent pitcher. Nor did the members of the nine regret their choice, for Dick pulled them out of several close games by his excellent twirling, which offset the errors made by his companions.

CHAPTER XXV

OFF TO CAMP

"Hurray!" yelled Paul Drew one afternoon, as he fairly jumped into the room which he and Dick shared.

"What's the matter?" asked his chum.

"Matter? Why, lots. You've passed, and so have I. We're going to be corporals from now on. That's for making good records in the spring examinations. Dutton and Hale are to be majors, I heard. I'm glad for Hale's sake, but it's going to be bad for us to have Dutton given so much authority."

"Why?"

"Because he'll lord it over us worse than ever. Well, it can't be helped. And there's more good news. Get up and have a war dance, you old buzzard!"

"Hold on!" cried Dick protestingly, as Paul yanked him from the easy chair. "What's up?"

"Lots. We're going to camp!"

"Camp?"

"Yes; it's just been announced. We're to go and spend one week under canvas; with no lessons to worry about, and lots of chance to skylark and have fun."

"I guess there'll be instructions in tactics, and recitations, won't there?" asked Dick. "It won't be all pie."

"Oh, of course we'll have to do some studying, I think."

"Of course. We'll have to tell what we'd do if, leading a small force of men, we happened to meet with an overwhelming army in a mountain pass, hemmed in on every side."

"I'd surrender," said Paul, with a laugh.

"I wouldn't; I'd fight," said Dick grimly, and he squared his jaw after the manner of Grit, his bulldog.

"Oh, well, we'll have lots of sport," went on Paul. "Of course it's for military instruction we're going, but I think we can manage to slip in a good time now and again."

"Sure," replied Dick, his eyes brightening. "When do we go?"

"Day after to-morrow. Orders are to get our kits in shape. We're to go in light marching order. The tents and grub will be carried in a wagon."

"That's good. I hate to pack my house, and all I want to eat, on my back."

The two chums fell to discussing the pleasant prospects ahead of them, some of the freshman cadets in neighboring rooms dropping in occasionally to get points on what to do and how to do it.

They were interrupted by a knock on Dick's door, and for a moment the buzz of voices ceased, as if the owners had been caught in some breach of the rules. Then, as the whistled strains of "In the Prison Cell I Sit," came to them, Dick exclaimed:

"It's Toots. Come on in, you old Horse Marine."

Toots entered, whistling a reveille with great precision.

"Major Webster wants to see you, Mr. Hamilton," he said, saluting.

"Me?" repeated Dick.

"Yes. In his office."

"You're in for a wigging," consoled Paul.

"Court martial for yours," added 'Gene Graham.

"No, I'm going to be promoted to take entire command of the camp," said Dick with a laugh as he went out. He had come nearer the truth than he thought in his jesting words. He saluted the major, who returned it, and bade him be seated.

"Ah, Hamilton, by the way, before I forget it, let me say that I haven't heard anything about that marksman's medal yet," said Major Webster, referring to the one that had fallen from the pocket of Toots. "When I hear anything I'll let you know. But that wasn't why I sent for you."

Dick thought it couldn't be anything serious, or the major wouldn't have begun in this fashion, so he waited.

"I have been looking up your record, Hamilton," went on the old soldier, "and I am very much pleased with it. So much so, in fact, that I am going to promote you, temporarily, and give you a command."

Dick's heart began to beat rapidly.

"During this encampment," went on the major, "we wish the new cadets to get a good idea of the value of military training, and what this academy stands for. I think that by this plan of mine they will gain more knowledge in a week than they otherwise would in two months. Now I am going to take all the cadets who recently arrived and form them into two companies. One you will have entire charge of, as captain. The other I will select a captain for. Yours will be known as Number One Company, to distinguish it from the regular lettered commands I want you to give the freshmen as good an idea as you can of what a military life here means."

"What am I to do?" asked Dick.

"Take entire charge of them. See that they are shown everything, from how to load a gun, vault upon a horse, put up a tent, build a camp fire, mount guard and so on. At the end of the week's camp we are going to have a sham battle."

"A sham battle?"

"Yes, off in the woods. The cadets will be divided into two armies, and we will play the war game just as the regulars and volunteers do. In a sense the lads in your care will be volunteers, and perhaps they will do better than the regular cadets. That part is up to you."

Dick resolved that if he could bring it about his company would gain some honors.

"Your command will be part of the fighting force in the sham battle," went on the major, "and it will depend on yourself how they behave. The rules of the sham battle will be announced later, but I want you to get ready for your shoulder straps," and he smiled at our hero.

"Well," thought Dick, as he left the major a little later, "I got to a captain's stripes before I knew it—but it won't last very long," he added, somewhat regretfully.

Dick thought ruefully that, even with this temporary promotion, he was hardly fulfilling the conditions of his mother's will. He was certainly not popular with the great body of students, and he began worrying lest he be sent to his Uncle Ezra. As he walked back to his room, he recalled a letter he had received from his father that day, stating that Mr. Hamilton would remain abroad longer than he had originally planned.

"It doesn't look as if I was going to make good," thought Dick, gloomily, as he entered his apartment.

"What was it?" asked his chums eagerly, as he came back.

Dick told them.

"A sham battle!" cried Paul. "That's the stuff! Hold me down, somebody, or I'll stand on my head, and if I do I'll split my new uniform. Hold me, somebody, do."

"I will," volunteered 'Gene Graham, and he obligingly tilted Paul up, so that he turned a neat summersault over his bed.

"I guess that'll hold you for a few moments," observed Stanley Booker. "Now tell us more about it, Dick."

Which the young millionaire proceeded to do.

Never was there such excitement in Kentfield academy as when it became known that, in addition to the camp there was to be a sham battle. On every side was heard talk of ambuscades, skirmishing parties, rear attacks, retrograde movements, waiting for reinforcements, deploys and bases of supplies.

Dutton sneered openly when he heard of Dick's promotion.

"I suppose he thinks he'll do wonders with those freshies," he said. "Maybe he hopes he'll win the battle by coming up with them as reinforcements."

"Well a small force has turned the tide more than once, Dutton," Allen Rutledge reminded him.

"I don't think Hamilton can do it, though," was the reply of the bully.

The start for camp was made on a bright, sunny morning, and the line of cadets, in field uniforms, with their guns over their shoulders, the sun glinting from the polished barrels, made an inspiring picture.

"Isn't this glorious?" said Dick to Paul, near whom he was marching.

"Silence in the ranks!" snapped Major Dutton, though there was no need for the command.

CHAPTER XXVI

THE SHAM BATTLE

Forward marched the cadets, keeping step to the lively air of the fifes, and the accompanying rattle and boom of the drums. But regular formation and step were not maintained for long, only until the young soldiers were on the main road, when they were allowed to break step, and proceed as they pleased, the companies, however, keeping together.

It was an all day's tramp to camp, and they stopped midway on the road for lunch, the baggage wagons having been halted while the regular cooks of the academy, who had been taken along, prepared the meal.

"Wait until we get the tents up," said Dick, "then we'll have some fun. Nothing like life under canvas in the summer."

"Right, Captain Dick," replied Paul, trying to talk with part of a chicken sandwich in his mouth. Dick had not yet assumed his new command, but would as soon as camp was pitched.

They got to the place about five o'clock, and found that the tents had been unloaded from the wagons, and that the cooks had their white shelter already set up, and were preparing supper.

"Now, boys," said Major Webster, "I want to see how soldierly you can do things. You have had considerable practice in putting up tents, at least you older cadets have; now let's see how you have profited by your instruction."

In a short time the scene was one of great activity. Cadets were straightening out folds of canvas, laying out ropes, driving in tent pegs and, in less than half an hour, where there had been a green field, it was now dotted with spotless white peaked-roof houses of canvas.

"Very well done," complimented Colonel Masterly, who came out of the headquarters tent to look at the sight. "Very fine, indeed, major."

"Yes, I think they did well."

The next work was to dig a trench about each tent so that rain water could not settle about it, and this was quickly accomplished. This done the camp had a fine appearance, the tents being arranged in rows or company "streets."

By this time supper was announced, and the way the cadets put away the good things which the cooks had provided made those servants open their eyes. They were used to hungry boys eating, but they almost forgot to allow for the extra appetites created by work in the open air. It was some time since a general camp had been held at the academy.

After guard mount, sentinels were posted and orders given that no cadet would be allowed to leave camp. In spite of this some of Dutton's crowd, including himself, ran the guard that night and were nearly caught. However, this was to be expected, and it was considered no great crime.

The next day Dick was given charge of forty freshmen, and he took great delight in starting their instruction. There were drills to attend, lessons in tactics to learn, the best method to observe on a march, and illustrations given in artillery firing, for several field pieces had been brought along to use in the sham battle.

Cavalry exercises occupied a part of every day, and though the cadets had plenty of leisure they found that their time was pretty fully occupied, for Colonel Masterly and his staff wanted practical benefit to be derived from the camp life. Target practice in the open proved to many a cadet who had done well on the ranges that he had plenty yet to learn.

"I wish they'd hurry up and have that sham battle," remarked Paul to Dick one night. "Heard anything about it?"

"It takes place to-morrow," replied our hero. "Blank ammunition will be served out the first thing in the morning, and final instructions given. My company is to form part of the attacking party."

"That's good. I wonder where my bunch will be stationed? I wish I was an officer."

"It will come in time. You're to be on the defense, I believe. So is the company of freshmen that Foraker has charge of."

"Well, it won't make much difference. I'll not fire on you, if I can help it."

"That's good."

The plan for the sham battle was announced the next morning, after each cadet had been supplied with many rounds of blank cartridges. The young soldiers were divided into two equal commands. Somewhat to Dick's disgust Major Dutton was given charge of the attacking party, of which the millionaire's son and his young lads formed a part. Harry Hale, the football coach, who had also been elected a major, was to be on the defensive. The latter army was to occupy a wooded hill, back of the camp. At the foot of it ran a small stream, and to get at the defenders of the mound the attacking party would have to build a temporary bridge, which work was included in the instruction imparted at the academy.

To cover this operation, the artillery of the attacking party would be brought up, but, at the same time, the field pieces of the defenders might pour a devastating fire on the bridge builders from above.

The holders of the hill were to be stationed at the rear limits of it, while the attackers were to start their march about two miles from the foot of the slope. It was figured out that if the defenders could bring up their artillery, and other forces, and attack the enemy before a bridge could be built across the stream, the holders of the hill would win the battle. On the other hand, if the attackers could succeed in getting a body of cadets across the stream before a heavy artillery or rifle fire could be poured into them, they would win. The promptness of firing, the number of shots and general quickness were to count.

At the appointed time, Major Hale and his force took possession of the hill, and Major Dutton led his army two miles back, on the plain in front of it.

Dutton issued his orders.

"We'll try to surprise them," he said to his young officers. "We'll swing around in a half circle, and instead of building the bridge at the easiest place to cross the stream we'll try it farther down. They won't suspect that we'll come there, and we'll gain some time."

"But they'll have their pickets out," observed Russell Glen. "They'll see us."

"I'll send some of you to another point to pretend to build a bridge," decided Dutton. "That'll draw their fire, and they'll start their artillery toward that place. Before they find out that it's only a bluff we'll have the real bridge half done."

As the cadets had a record of building a thirty-foot bridge of the "A" style inside of four minutes, it seemed that Dutton's plan might be a good one.

"How are you going to carry the planks and spars for the bridge?" asked Glen. "On the field piece carriages?"

"No, we'll carry them ourselves. We can close up ranks so they won't see the boards."

This looked like a good plan, and the cadets made ready to carry it out.

"Hamilton," said Dutton sharply to our hero, "you'll take the rear guard, and stay there until you get orders to come up."

This was rather hard on Dick. It practically put him and his freshmen out of the battle, unless Dutton should order them to the front, and he was not very likely to do this. Still Dick could not object, and he made the best of it.

"Won't we see any of the fighting?" asked one of his command.

"Maybe so," replied the young millionaire. "They may need us for reinforcements."

Dick could not help but give Dutton credit for making his plans well. The young major led his men to the designated point, taking advantage of such inequalities of the ground as there were to conceal his movements. The ropes, beams and planks for the bridge were distributed among the cadets, several of them being required to carry the heavier pieces. The strongest lads were used for this work, and their rifles were taken in charge by their less-burdened comrades.

Then, when all was in readiness, Dutton gave the command to advance. He led the way, at the head of a company of infantry, while back of that came his cavalry force, and to the rear of that was massed his artillery, while Dick led the rear guard of freshmen.

Straight at the hill advanced the attacking army, while from convenient points Colonel Masterly and his staff of officers watched to decide who won.

"Skirmishers, advance!" ordered Dutton, and several cadets detached themselves from the cavalry and rode forward. As they approached there were puffs of white smoke from the slope of the hill, and the sharp crack of rifles announced that the pickets of Major Hale's force were on the alert. The skirmishers returned the fire, and then galloped back to report.

"They're waiting for us," Dutton was informed.

"So I see," he replied. "Now, then, we'll halt here a moment. You fellows that are to pretend to build the bridge, get ready to rush when I give the word. I'll send one field piece as if to cover your movements. Are you all ready there, Stiver?" for Lieutenant Stiver, with whom Dutton had again gotten on friendly terms, was to lead the fake movement.

"All ready," was the answer.

"Then go!"

Out from the attacking force rushed a squad of cadets, bearing light planks. Of course, from the hill, it looked as if they were the advance guard of bridge builders. Particularly when there dashed out a field piece, drawn by galloping horses.

As the cadets approached the bank of the stream, and began to arrange their planks, the lads in charge of the cannon quickly wheeled it, unlimbered and fired the first shot. There was a white puff of smoke, a burst of flame, and a great bang went rattling and echoing among the hills. The battle had opened.

As Dutton had expected, his ruse deceived Hale. The latter quickly ordered up his entire artillery to shell the intrepid bridge builders. Dutton, watching through a field glass, saw the approach of the cannon.

"Forward march!" he cried to his main command. "Double quick!"

Quickness was everything now. Off they started, the real bridge builders and nearly his entire force, including Dick and his youngsters in the rear.

They circled around a turn in the stream, and, for a time, were out of sight of the small force left to bear the attack.

"Build the bridge here!" ordered Dutton. "Lively now, boys. See if you can't break the record."

The cadets needed no urging. Two of them quickly plunged into the stream, and, partly swimming, partly wading, carried over some ropes. By means of these they pulled over spars and planks, which, when several of their companions hurriedly joined them, they proceeded to lash together. The same operation was going on among the cadets on the other side of the brook.

Two long spars were laid down on the ground, at right angles to the stream. At the further extremity of these spars a cross piece was lashed, projecting on either side. Ropes were attached to the projections, and the unconnected ends of the long spars, being held down to the ground by several lads, the others quickly raised the connected ends, just as a painter hoists a long ladder. The same thing took place on the farther side of the brook, and, when both squads were ready, the two parts of the bridge that were to form the two slanting sides of a double letter "A" were allowed to incline toward each other, from either side of the water, cadets having hold of the ropes, regulating and guiding the long spars. The big sticks met in mid air, over the centre of the stream, and, being well braced at the bottom, held. Then cadets climbed up on either side, and united them more firmly by lashing them.

Something like a double letter "A," but without the cross piece, now spanned the brook. Or, perhaps, it would be more correct to say that it was a double inverted "V." It was necessary to put on cross spars, and lay planks on these, or the artillery and cavalry could not get over. And, as there were no spars long enough to reach all the way across the stream, two sections had to be used on either side of the bridge. They were to be tied together, and supported at the centre, or place of joining, by long ropes, attached to the apex of the letter "A."

Though up to this time the main attacking party had not been fired on, they could not hope to escape much longer. Already puffs of white smoke from the hillside indicated that they had been seen by pickets. A minute later Dutton's trick was discovered, and Hale ordered his artillery to cease firing on the fake bridge builders, and to turn their attack on the others.

But Dutton was ready for this. He had his field pieces in position, and, as soon as he saw that his soldiers had the bridge well under way, he began shelling the defenders, who were rushing down the hill to the attack. The infantry also began to pour in a withering fire.

The ropes, by which the long spars had been lowered and inclined across the stream, now served as guys to hold them steady and in place, while the floor beams were being put in position.

"Lively!" cried Dutton. "They're making it too hot for us! We must cross soon, or we'll lose! They came at us quicker than I expected!"

Meanwhile the little force that had started to build the fake bridge had (theoretically) been killed.

Now the long floor timbers were in place, being supported at the centre by long ropes, hanging from the point of the "A," and the cadets were beginning to lay cross planks on them.

"Tell the cavalry to get ready to advance, to protect our crossing," ordered Dutton, to one of his captains, and the troop of lads on their restless steeds prepared to rush across the bridge at the first possible moment. It had only been a little over three minutes since the building of the structure was started, but a heavy artillery fire was being concentrated on the attackers, and, in accordance with instructions previously given, cadets began dropping out, being supposed to be killed.

Dutton's field pieces were pounding away, and there was a thick cloud of smoke, which partly concealed the movements of his cadets.

"Bridge is ready, major!" reported a smoke-begrimed lad, running up, and saluting. Then he hastened back to continue firing on Hale's soldiers.

"Advance, cavalry!" shouted Dutton. "Lively now! Charge!"

The horses, urged on by their shouting riders, thundered over the frail bridge. It trembled and swayed, but it supported them.

"Forward, the infantry!" cried the young major. "On the double quick! Here they come down the hill at you! Fire at will! Charge!"

Down the slope of the hill came rushing the defenders. Behind them thundered and rumbled their artillery, which was supporting their brave advance in the face of the enemy.

"Artillery, forward!" shouted Dutton, waving his sword, and hoping, by throwing his entire force suddenly upon Hale's army, to overpower it, and get in more shots than could his opponent. That meant he would win the battle.

"Shall I stay here?" cried Dick, for he had received no orders what to do with his force, and was still on the farther side of the bridge.

"Yes! Until I send for you, or you see that you are needed," called back Dutton. "I guess I can get along without you."

Louder roared the cannon; and the cracks of the rifles of the infantry, and the carbines of the cavalry, was like the explosion of pack after pack of giant firecrackers.

Then something happened. As the three field pieces rumbled across the bridge, there was an ominous cracking and splintering sound. Dutton heard it and turned back from his rush, which he had started on to be in readiness to lead the charge of his artillery. He saw the bridge swaying.

"Come on! Come on!" he cried, waving his sword. "Come on!"

But it was too late. The middle supporting ropes had slipped, and the bridge collapsed at the centre, letting horses, cannon and cadets down into the stream, which, fortunately, was not deep.

Dutton had, at one blow, lost all his artillery, while Hale's was advancing to annihilate him and his force. The boom of the defenders' field pieces sounded nearer and nearer, while their rifle fire became hotter than ever.

Dutton saw himself defeated by the inopportune collapse of the bridge, which had been insecurely lashed together. But he would not give up.

"Forward! Forward!" he cried. "Split up and attack 'em on both sides."

His cavalry and infantry rushed forward, firing as they ran. Dick Hamilton, left with his little body of troops on the other side of the stream, saw his opportunity.

"Quick!" he cried to his lads. "We'll go back and get the guns at the fake bridge. Then we'll pull it across and we'll see if we can execute a flank movement."

"That's the stuff!" cried some of the lads, who had begun to fear they would never get a chance to fire their rifles.

Dick led his men on the double quick to where the field piece, from which only a few shots had been fired, had been left. He saw a chance to turn defeat into victory.

CHAPTER XXVII

DICK WINS THE CONTEST

Dutton was desperate when he saw the most efficient arm of his little force thus wiped out. He did not turn back to help the cadets in charge of the horses and guns, however, as he knew they could look after themselves.

And this they did, though they had to cut the traces to get the horses loose from the guns, and then haul the field pieces out by hand. This took some time, and when the cannon were safe on the other shore they could not be used because the harness was cut and the horses could not pull them. Besides the guns had turned over and the working parts were all wet.

But Major Dutton had not yet given up. He divided his cavalry and infantry into two divisions, giving Captain Beeby charge of one, and taking the other himself.

Dutton took advantage of a little hollow which, for a few moments hindered the advance of the defenders, to execute this move, and he hoped to be able to turn the flank of Hale.

"Make as wide a swing as you can," he advised Beeby, "and maybe you can get to him before we have to give up," for according to the rules of the sham battle about half of Dutton's force was now wiped out. It showed his spirit when he was unwilling to send for Dick's reinforcements, but he decided he would not owe victory to the lad he hated, if he could help it.

Beeby got well away with his cadets before Hale and his forces appeared around a little mound on the big hill. Then, though it was hard work to handle his artillery there, the major of the defenders made a stand and gave pitched battle to the contingent led by Dutton.

For a time the fight waged furiously, but it was unequal, as Dutton had no cannon with which to reply to the bombardment he was suffering. Nor could his cavalry advance to good advantage up the slope, while Hale's had no difficulty in coming down.

"Now, if Beeby would only get there," thought Dutton, "we might win yet!"

Alas for his hopes! Hale had suspected some such movement, and had held back a reserve force. Skirmishers saw Beeby advancing through the woods, and gave the alarm. Then Hale brought up a field piece he had not yet used, and opened fire on Beeby's contingent, which Dutton hoped would have saved him. There was no help for it. He was on the point of ordering a retreat, as the only way of saving a part of his force. Still he had a considerable number of cadets left, and they had plenty of ammunition.

Meanwhile Dick and his freshmen cadets had not been idle. Under his directions they unhitched the six horses from the cannon, and, by attaching ropes to the piece they pulled it across the stream on a raft they improvised from the boards used to construct the fake bridge. Thus the piece was saved from getting wet. The fake bridge builders, who had (theoretically) been killed, offered no objection. They could take no further part in the battle.

"Who are the best riders?" asked Dick, and several lads modestly offered themselves.

"You'll be the cavalry," said the young commander. "You are only six, but you'll do for what I want, which is mostly bluff."

He gave the artillery horses to six lads, and bade them ride across the stream, which they easily did.

"Wade and swim for the rest of us," said Dick grimly. "Hold your rifles above your heads, for, though the cartridges are water-proof, it doesn't do the mechanism of a gun any good to get it wet. Lively now. We'll be too late if we don't hurry. They're keeping up quite a heavy artillery fire."

The eager cadets needed no urging. They crossed the stream in good order, not being observed by either Dutton's force, or by the defenders of the hill. On the other side Dick looked forthe easiest and best way of climbing the hill, and going to Dutton's aid.

He saw a sort of trail leading up, and, from the direction of the firing, he knew that he could, if undiscovered, take Hale on his left flank, Beeby having tried to turn the right unsuccessfully, though Dick did not know this then.

It was hard work urging the horses up the steep hill, and harder still for the cadets to drag up the field piece, and the limber filled with ammunition, little of which had been used. But they did it, and on they went.

Dick, coming out on a little projection, could see the battle in progress between Dutton and Hale. The latter had all but won, and the attackers were fast being driven back. They were a mere handful of cadets now, many having been "killed" by the merciless fire. Being "killed" in theory meant that a certain number had to drop out every minute, and could take no further part in the battle. Of course Hale had a number of soldiers "killed" also.

"Hurry!" cried Dick to his lads. "We're only just in time. A little farther and we'll plant the field piece and open fire. Then we'll charge down."

The lads dragged the cannon a few hundred feet farther up the hill. Then, screening it behind some bushes, Dick told off a number of cadets to work the gun, they having had previous practice.

"Ready!" he called, and to the surprise of Hale, no less than that of Dutton, the woods echoed to the report of artillery where none was supposed to be. A white puff of smoke on Hale's left flank told him that some movement was in progress over there. He was about to order one of his guns to reply to the unexpected bombardment, when there came a ringing shout from the same quarter, and, above the cheer, Dick Hamilton yelled:

"Charge!"

Down upon the all but victorious defenders of the hill rushed the little force of six cavalrymen. Behind them, leading about thirty cadets, who were as fresh as daisies, came Dick.

"Charge! Charge!" he yelled, and then he ordered the lads to open fire.

They did it with a will, for they had not had a chance to use their guns yet, and they were wild to do so.

What a fire they poured into the ranks of the defenders. How the one lone field piece, well screened by bushes, sent shell after shell (theoretically) screaming into the midst of the enemy.

Hale was all but demoralized. He had seen victory just within his grasp, and now he was attacked by fresh reinforcements. Dutton had been too much for him, after all, he thought.

As for Dutton, he hardly knew what to make of it. He could not understand how Dick had been able to lead up his forces, to execute a successful flank movement, and, above all, to bring a field piece to bear.

Hale was now in desperate straits. Encouraged by seeing reinforcements Dutton's men turned with cries of gladness to renew the attack. Hale tried to reply to them, but his ammunition was getting low. Closer in came Dick and his lads, pressing on Hale's flank. On the other side Beeby, with the few cadets he had left, returned to the attack. In front Dutton and a handful of soldiers poured in a fire. But Dick's was the fiercest, aided as it was by the cannon.

There was nothing for Hale to do but to retreat, and he had his bugler sound this mournful call. Up the hill he and his men went—what was left of them—while after them rushed Dick, now leading the attack.

"Surrender! Surrender!" cried Dutton. "We've got you!"

"I guess you have," admitted Hale. "But if Hamilton hadn't come when he did there'd been a different story."

Dutton did not reply, nor did he glance at Dick, who, seeing that the battle was over, had ordered his command to cease firing. But, though Major Dutton did not acknowledge that Dick had saved the day, he knew it, and so did his men.

Major Webster, however, did not withhold his praise.

"Hamilton, you did splendidly!" he cried enthusiastically. "That was a master stroke to ford the stream, take the gun over, and use the horses for cavalry. Major Dutton, thanks to Captain Hamilton, your forces have the honor of having won the sham battle. I congratulate you. I am proud of my cadets, even the losers."

"Three cheers for Major Hale!" called Dutton, who was politic, if a bully.

The camp rang with the shouts.

"Now three cheers for Major Dutton!" called Hale, and the huzzahs were louder than before, for Dutton had a magnetic attractiveness in spite of his mean ways with those whom he did not like.

"Three cheers for Captain Hamilton!" called Paul Drew, but, though Dick's freshmen nearly yelled the tops of their heads off, the cheer for our hero was noticeably weaker than either of the two preceding ones.

Dick smiled grimly, but he knew he had done good work that day.

CHAPTER XXVIII

UNCLE EZRA AT KENTFIELD

The rest of that day, and far into the night, ignoring the warning of tattoo and taps, the cadets discussed the sham battle. It had been a glorious affair, and they fought it all over again in their tents, the defeated ones explaining that if "this" had happened, "that" wouldn't have taken place.

"But for all that, you can't deny but that Dick saved the day for Dutton," argued Paul.

"He certainly did," was the general reply.

The battle practically ended the military instruction at camp. The next day was devoted to resting and light drills. Several lads had received severe sprains or bruises, due to their haste or enthusiasm, and one horse had a cut leg caused by the accident to the bridge.

There was some disposition to criticize Dutton for not seeing that the structure was secure before sending his artillery over, but Major Webster declared that as no serious accident had resulted no fault could be found. As for the young major it was bitter for him to have to admit, as he grudgingly did, that he would have failed but for Dick Hamilton.

Another day spent in camp, when all discipline was relaxed, and the cadets were allowed to do about as they pleased, brought the outing to a close. Then all sorts of tricks were played, and more than one crowd of freshmen found their tent coming down unexpectedly about their heads that night, as the mischief makers loosened the pegs.

Bright and early the next morning the tents were struck, the baggage was loaded into the wagons, and the "hike" to the academy was begun. The cadets fell into line, and with swinging step, to the tune of "The Girl I Left Behind Me," paraded off the camping ground.

It was rather hard to settle down again to the grind of lessons, but Colonel Masterly and his colleague knew how to handle boys, and in between study and recitation periods were drills and cavalry and infantry exercises so that gradually the routine was resumed again, and every one felt better for the outing.

One day, as Dick and Paul came in from the campus, they saw a notice on the bulletin board. It was to the effect that candidates for the 'Varsity baseball team would report in the gymnasium that night.

"That's the stuff!" cried Dick enthusiastically.

"Are you going to play?" asked Paul.

"Sure. Why not?"

"Well, you didn't get much show at football last year."

"Can't help it. I may this time."

"Dutton is just as much against you as ever."

"I know it, but I may get a chance just the same. I'm going to begin training, and I'll keep at it until the last game."

Dick was as good as his word. He rather hoped he might make the regular nine, but he learned that Dutton and his set were against him, and the best he could do was to be named as a substitute shortstop.

The season opened rather badly for Kentfield, for they lost the first game, and that against a small college team. It was because Captain Rutledge was so confident that he did not play his men with any vim, and several bad fumbles cost them the game.

They won the first of the championship contests with Mooretown academy, and lost the second, making it a tie, and so the third game, which would be played at Kentfield that spring, would be an important and the deciding one.

Dick got an opportunity to play on the regular team once during the last few innings, but as the game, which was with a small college, was won by the cadets before he went into it, his performance did not receive much credit.

"If I only get a chance to play against Mooretown," he said to Paul, "I'll be satisfied. Anyhow, I'm one of the subs."

It was the day of the great and deciding game with Mooretown. Dick was struggling into his trousers and blouse in his room, when Toots brought him word that there was a visitor for him in the reception room.

"Who is it, Toots?" he asked. "I haven't much time. Most of the fellows are already on the diamond."

"He says his name is Honeybee, as near as I can make out."

"Honeybee," repeated Dick, much puzzled. "Oh, it must be Larabee. It's my Uncle Ezra!"

Then a look of annoyance came over his face.

"If I go down to see him he'll keep me from the game," he thought. "I haven't any time to spare. He'll lecture me about the waste of time in playing baseball, or the danger of it, or something like that. Or he may want me to show him around the academy. No, he's not likely to do that, for fear he'd wear out his shoes. I wonder what in the world he can want, anyhow? But if I see him now I'll never get a chance to play. I'll not see him."

"Toots," he said, "tell my uncle that I have an important engagement, and ask him to wait until I come back."

"All right, Mr. Hamilton," replied the janitor. "Shall I tell him what it is? Maybe he'd like to see the game," and Toots softly whistled "Just Before the Battle, Mother."

"No! No! Don't tell him!" exclaimed Dick. "He thinks baseball is wicked. Just say— say anything you like except that. I'll come back as soon as the game's over—if I'm alive. He won't mind waiting. It will give him a chance to think."

Which perhaps was not exactly polite on Dick's part. He hurried off, leaving Uncle Ezra in the reception room, wondering what important business his nephew had that kept him so long. And, by not seeing his Uncle Ezra, Dick missed hearing a bit of news that was destined to make a great change in his affairs. But he heard it later, as you will see.

While our hero was on his way to the field, hoping that he would get a chance to play, Uncle Ezra sat in the reception room. He was not very impatient at the delay. As Dick had said, it gave him a chance to think.

Presently the door opened, and Russell Glen looked in the apartment. He was in search of Dutton, having been told the young major was there. Not seeing his friend, he was about to withdraw, with an apology for having disturbed Mr. Larabee.

"Are you one of the students here?" asked Dick's uncle, who was getting rather tired waiting.

"Yes. I'm in my second year."

"Ah, then you must know my nephew, Richard Hamilton?"

"Oh, yes, I know Dick."

"Richard is his proper name," corrected Mr. Larabee stiffly.

Glen nodded, and was about to go out.

"If you see him, I wish you would tell him to hurry," went on Mr. Larabee. "I have been waiting for some time for him, but he sent word that he had an important engagement, and would see me later."

Glen guessed what the "engagement" was, so he merely nodded.

"I want to see him very particularly," continued the aged man, "as I have some important news for him. It may make a great difference in his life. In fact, I'm sure it will."

Glen opened his eyes at this, and decided not to go just yet.

"Has some one left him some more millions?" he asked in a joking tone.

"Far from it," said Mr. Larabee in solemn accents.

"Eh?" asked Glen, wondering what was coming.

"I always said it was foolish for my sister to leave Richard so much money," went on Mr. Larabee severely, "and I told Mortimer Hamilton that he was risking his money to go to Europe. Now, what I said would happen has happened."

"Is Mr. Hamilton in trouble?" asked Glen, not a little rejoiced to find that difficulties were in store for Dick.

"Well, I'd call it trouble to lose nearly all my fortune. But it serves Mortimer right, and Richard also."

"Has Mr. Hamilton lost his money?" inquired Glen, coming closer to Mr. Larabee.

"Practically so."

"And Dick?"

"A large part of his is gone also. It was invested with Mr. Hamilton's. I received word of it yesterday, and I hurried to come here and tell him. A New York bank, in which Mr. Hamilton was largely interested, and in which were most of Dick's funds, as well his father's, has failed."

"Then Mr. Hamilton isn't a millionaire any longer?"

"I fear not."

"And Dick?" asked Glen eagerly.

"He has very little left."

"Whew!" whistled the cadet. This would be news indeed to the students. He must hasten and tell them.

"That's what I came to see my nephew about," went on Mr. Larabee. "I want him to come away from this expensive school, and live with me until his father returns. Oh, the money that young man has wasted! It is awful! Terrible!" and Uncle Ezra seemed about to faint with the horror of it.

"Shall I find Dick for you?" asked Glen.

"I wish you would, young man. I want to tell him this news, and take him back with me. I have a return ticket on the railroad, and if I stay over night it will be no good. Besides I am afraid my hired man will use kerosene oil in starting the fire if I am not home by morning, and he might burn down the house. One can not be too careful of money. Mortimer and my nephew are a terrible example. Find him for me, if you will, please."

"I will," promised Glen, hurrying away. "My word!" he exclaimed as he ran out on the campus. "Hamilton's money all gone! Then he's no better than the rest of us now. He'll come down a peg or two."

Considering that Dick had never tried to hang himself on a "peg," this seemed a useless as well as cruel remark.

"I wish I had borrowed a hundred from him yesterday, instead of fifty," mused Glen, as he hurried on toward the baseball field. As he neared it he heard shouts and cheers.

"The game's started," he exclaimed, as he broke into a run.

CHAPTER XXIX

DICK'S GREAT RUN

Dick Hamilton hurried across to the players' bench, tightening his belt as he ran.

"If I only get a chance to play," he kept thinking. "I don't care what happens after that, nor what Uncle Ezra may want."

The game soon started, and it began to look bad for Kentfield, for the outfielders made several costly errors, and at the ending of the sixth inning the score was eight to three, in favor of Mooretown.

"Looks rather bad," said Captain Rutledge to the coach.

"Nonsense," replied Hale. "You can win yet. Take a brace, that's all."

Kentfield had elected to be last at the bat, and, in the beginning of the seventh inning, when Mooretown was up, Perkins, the regular short stop, split his hand in stopping a "hot" ball. The other players gathered about him.

"I guess it's all up with us now," remarked Dutton, from his seat in the grandstand. "We haven't got anyone who can play like Perkins. Hamilton is green. Our goose is cooked."

"Say, I've got some news about Hamilton," spoke Russell Glen, worming his way to Dutton's side, during the lull in the contest following the injury of Perkins.

"I don't care. I want to see how this game is coming out."

Perkins walked to the bench, blood dripping from his hand.

"Hamilton!" cried Captain Rutledge, and Dick sprang from the bench, pulling off his sweater. His chance had come.

"Hamilton's going to play," said Dutton. "Oh, what a score they'll roll up against us! They'll knock all their balls at him, and he'll miss them. What were you saying about Hamilton?" he went on, turning to Glen. "This is tough luck, though!"

"Hamilton has lost all his money!" cried Glen, and his tone seemed to show that he relished the news.

"No!"

"Fact. His uncle told me," and Glen related the story he had received from Mr. Larabee.

Dutton was greatly surprised, and so were several other cadets who overheard what Glen had said. But there was little time to speculate on it, as the game was under way again.

Whether it was Dick's presence at shortstop, or because the other players on his team braced up, was not evident. At any rate, Mooretown was held down to a goose egg in that inning, and when it came the turn of Kentfield to show what the nine could do in the ending of the seventh inning, there were three runs to the credit of the cadets, Dick having made one.

"The score is six to eight!" murmured Glen to Dutton. "Hamilton isn't doing so bad."

"No, but he would if he knew all his money was gone, I guess."

"Maybe we ought to tell him," suggested the sporty student.

"I wish I could," murmured Dutton.

The game went on fiercely. It was nip and tuck all the while now, for Kentfield's chances had improved wonderfully, and they were fighting hard to win.

In the eighth inning neither side scored. There was an anxious look on the faces of all the players as the ninth opened. Mooretown could afford to smile, however, as she was still two runs ahead. At first it looked as if she would pile up several more tallies on this score, for the Kentfield pitcher gave two men their bases on balls, and the next man got to first on an easy fly.

A heavy hitter was up next, and at the first crack he sent a "hot liner" straight at Dick. Our hero did not flinch, though the impact was terrific. He caught the ball squarely, and the batter was out. Then, by a neat double play, Dick and the third baseman put out another man who was trying to steal home.

The next batter struck out, retiring Mooretown without a run, but still leaving them two ahead.

"Now, fellows, we must show them what we're made of!" cried the captain. "We want three runs this inning!"

Captain Rutledge did his share by getting one, and another was brought in by a narrow margin, tying the score.

"One to win!" cried the coach.

"Hamilton up!" announced the score keeper.

"And two out!" added Dutton to Glen. "He can never do it. We're dumped already."

Dick took his place at the plate. It was a trying ordeal for a substitute player, and the eyes of all the spectators were upon him. The result of the game, in a great measure, depended on him. If he did not get the winning run, it meant that the game would go another inning, and the chances of Kentfield would not be improved. For their pitcher's arm was going "back on him," and Mooretown's man was still good for much twirling.

Amid a silence that was almost painful, Dick waited for the first ball. It came, but he did not move his bat.

"One strike!" called the umpire, and there was something like a groan among the Kentfield players.

The next was a ball, and the following one looked as if it was going fairly over the plate. But Dick did not attempt to hit it.

"Two strikes!"

It was like a death knell.

"He's cutting it pretty fine," murmured the captain nervously.

"Hamilton's all right," said Coach Hale confidently.

A moment later there came a resounding crack, as Dick's bat met the ball fairly. The horsehide went up in a graceful curve, and then sailed far out toward right field.

"Go on! Go on! Go on!" yelled Captain Rutledge, but his voice was lost in the roar that greeted Dick's hit. The young millionaire was leaping toward first base, while the right fielder was sprinting after the ball.

"A home run! A home run!" begged the coach, and it looked as if Dick would do it.

He got to third, and started for home. The fielder had the ball by this time, and relayed it to second. The man there threw it to third just as Dick left. Possibly it was an error of judgment, but Dick kept on. He could distinguish no coaching instructions now above the yells, though Hale was calling to him to remain on the bag. But Dick kept on.

Then, by some curious chance, the third baseman, instead of sending the ball home, held it in his hand, and raced after Dick. It was a contest of legs now. The baseman ignored the demands of the catcher to throw the ball, and leaped after Dick, who ran as he had never run before. He saw a vision of the game won, and, though his breath was coming in labored gasps, he did not stop. There was a mist before his eyes. His legs were tottering.

"Jove! But he can run!" whispered Dutton. "I never saw anything like it!"

"You bet!" agreed Glen fervidly.

On and on ran Dick. One quick glance over his shoulder showed him the baseman at his heels. He expected every moment to see the catcher get the ball, and put him out. But the horsehide did not come, and, the next instant, when Dick felt as if he could not go another inch, or draw another breath, he dropped, and slid home in a cloud of dust.

"Safe!" cried the umpire, and, as he spoke, the baseman, realizing the proper play, threw the ball. But it was too late. Dick had brought in the winning run.

"Wow! Wow! Wow! Hamilton! Hamilton! Hamilton! Whoop!" yelled the frenzied players. Above their shouts could be heard the shrill cries of many girls.

From the stands burst forth mighty cheers. A crowd of the cadet players surrounded Dick and would have carried him on their shoulders had he allowed them. They patted him on the back, and even punched him in their uncontrollable joy.

"Hamilton, you're entitled to the thanks of the entire school!" cried Coach Hale, rushing up, and wringing Dick's hand.

"We never could have won but for you!" admitted the captain. "Wow! but it was a fierce game!" and he sat down on the grass to recover his wind, after his lusty cheers.

They escorted Dick back to the dressing room in a sort of triumphal procession, scores of cadets pouring from the stands to join it. Never did a hero takes his honors more modestly. It was enough for Dick that he had helped win the victory, and he saw coming to him now what he had waited nearly a year for—fellowship.

Through the throng came Dutton and Glen.

"I say, Hamilton," called Glen, "your uncle's waiting for you."

"I know it," answered Dick. "But I couldn't talk to him until after the game."

"He's got news for you—bad news," went on Glen, with the relish some persons seem to take in telling of calamities.

"What is it?" inquired Dick, alarmed by the cadet's words and manner.

"Your father's fortune is wiped out, and so's yours! The New York bank has failed!"

For an instant Dick stared at the speaker. Then a changed look came over his face. He stepped forward, his suit covered with dirt, his face bleeding from a scratch, and still panting from his great run.

"My fortune lost?" he said. "I don't care a hang! We've won the game!"

There was a moment of silence so surprised were the cadets at the manner in which Dick took the news. Then Glen cried out:

"My word, but you're plucky! Three cheers for Hamilton—who used to be a millionaire—but isn't any longer," he added, and Dick's ears rang with the joyous shouts.

CHAPTER XXX

A BROADSWORD COMBAT

"Well, Nephew Richard, I've been waiting some time for you," said Uncle Ezra Larabee a little later, when Dick, having gotten out of his suit and donned his cadet uniform, went into the reception room. "I've been here for some time, and very likely I've lost my train, but I couldn't go back without seeing you."

"I'm sorry I kept you so long, Uncle Ezra," replied Dick, "but you see I was in a baseball game, and I couldn't leave until we won. It was very important to win."

"Stuff and nonsense!" exclaimed the old man. "Baseball is a dangerous and wicked game. It leads to all sorts of trouble. When I was a boy we played such sensible games as tag and blind-man's buff. Baseball! The idea!"

"The cadets of Kentfield would look pretty playing tag," thought Dick, but he did not say anything.

"I have some bad news for you, Nephew Richard," went on Uncle Ezra. "I suppose you wonder what it is."

"I know."

"You know?"

"Yes, Glen told me."

"Oh, he must be the young man whom I was talking to. Well, I regret very much to be the bearer of such ill tidings," went on Mr. Larabee, "but, if you are hoping that it is not true, you are much mistaken. I received word from New York yesterday that the bank in which was most of your father's wealth, as well as your own, which your mother, my sister, so foolishly left you——"

"Sir!" cried Dick, for he could not bear to hear his mother spoken of in that way.

"Well, I think it foolish to leave a youth so much money," said Mr. Larabee, "and now my judgment is confirmed. You are no longer a millionaire."

"I don't know as I care much," said Dick coolly. "My money didn't do as much as I expected it would."

"Foolish, perverse youth," murmured his uncle. "But you must make a change in your plans. You can no longer stay at this expensive school. You had better pack up your things and come home with me to Dankville. I will look after you until your father comes home from Europe. Doubtless I may be able to get you a position in a woolen mill in which I am interested. If you hurry we can take the late train, and I will be able to use the excursion ticket I bought."

Dick considered matters a moment. Then he said:

"I don't think I'll go with you, Uncle Ezra."

"Not go with me? Why, what will you do?"

"Stay here and finish out the spring term. I'm just beginning to enjoy himself. There are only a few weeks left."

"But how can you? You have very little, if any, money."

"My tuition and board are paid up to the end of this term," said Dick calmly. "I have considerable money on deposit in the Kentfield bank, that I drew out from my funds at Hamilton Corners, when I came here. That will last me for some time. I think I prefer staying here to going back to—to Dankville."

"Well, of all the foolish, idiotic, senseless, rash proceedings I ever heard of!" exclaimed Uncle Ezra. "The idea! You will stay here and use up what little money is saved from the wreck of your fortune! Why, maybe you could get a rebate on what has been paid for board and tuition."

"I shouldn't think of asking for it," said Dick. "No, I think I'll stick it out here."

There was a movement at the door, and something came into the room, something that slid up to Dick, and began wiggling at his feet.

"Quiet, Grit, old boy," he said.

"Is that your bulldog?" asked Uncle Ezra.

"Yes; he was too lonesome at home without me, so I sent for him. He stays in the stable."

"Another foolish and useless expense," murmured the old man. "Oh, what is the world coming to!"

Dick didn't know, so he didn't answer.

"Think well," went on Mr. Larabee. "You had better come home with me. I can get you work in the woolen mill."

"I'll stay here," replied Dick firmly.

"Then I wash my hands of you!" exclaimed the aged man. "Never appeal to me for help! I am done with you! Of all the foolish, thoughtless, rash youths I ever met, you are the worst; and your father——"

What Mr. Larabee would have said about Mr. Hamilton he never finished, for Grit, hearing the voice of a man he considered his enemy, made a rush from under the table where he was lying, and growled as though he was going to sample Uncle Ezra's legs.

"Take that brute away!" exclaimed Dick's crabbed relative, but before the order could be executed Mr. Larabee turned and fled from the room, Grit pursuing him as far as the hall.

"I guess we've seen the last of him for a while," mused Dick. "Eh, Grit, old boy?"

The bulldog nearly shook off his stump of a tail.

"Well, I guess I had better write to dad, and find out how bad things really are," he went on. "Still, there's no use worrying. I got along all right before I knew I was a millionaire, and I guess I can now when I'm not."

Someone looked in the reception room. It was Glen.

"I say, Hamilton," he remarked, "the boys are looking all over for you. They want you to lead a procession. We're going to have a grand celebration, burn the uniforms, and break training to celebrate the victory. Hurry up!"

"This is worth losing one's money for," thought Dick, as he took his place at the head of the procession of merry, shouting, laughing cadets. "I'm getting to be popular, I guess."

Indeed, whether it was his victory on the diamond or the loss of his money, it would be hard to say, but, at any rate, more cadets made friends with Dick that night than had done so in his whole previous time at Kentfield.

But though Dick had won the hearts of the baseball nine and their friends, he was still far from being one of the really popular lads in the school. Dutton and his cronies held aloof from him, and many followed their example.

But, unexpectedly, there came a great change in Dick's life, and Dutton was partly responsible for it. Dick and some of his companions were at broadsword exercise on horseback one day, while, on the farther side of the cavalry plain, there was a class drilling in artillery, under the direction of Dutton. Dick was fencing with Lyndon Butler, when suddenly Dutton's steed, frightened by the discharge of a cannon near it, reared, throwing the young major off.

Dutton's foot caught in the stirrup, and he was dragged along, unable to release himself, while six artillery horses, drawing a heavy gun, dashed down the field and seemed about to collide with the youthful major's animal.

Dick saw a chance to save his enemy, and turned his horse quickly, to make a dash. So rapid was his movement that Butler's sword gave him a gash in the face, Dick forgetting, in the excitement of the moment, to guard himself. With the blood streaming from a cut on his cheek Dick urged his horse at a gallop until he had caught Dutton's runaway mount. He did it only just in time, for, as he pulled the beast, still dragging the young major, to one side, the artillery steeds dashed over the spot. Dutton would have been killed but for Dick's prompt act.

Major Webster rode up quickly, and was glad to find that neither Dick nor Dutton was seriously hurt.

"Who caught my horse?" asked Dutton, as he struggled to his feet. "The last I remember was seeing him running toward the artillery animals, and I made up my mind there'd be quite a smash when they met."

"They didn't meet, thanks to Dick Hamilton," said the elderly major. "He stopped your horse just in time."

"And got a nasty cut into the bargain," added another cadet.

Dick was beginning to feel a trifle dizzy. He turned aside. Dutton took a step forward, in spite of his strained ankle.

"Hamilton," he said, and there was a husky note in his voice.

Dick turned back.

"Hamilton—I—er—I—I—will you shake hands?" asked Dutton suddenly, and he seemed much affected.

Dick grasped the outstretched hand, and the two, one of whom had been an unrelenting enemy of the other, looked into each other's eyes.

"Hamilton," went on Dutton, still holding Dick's hand, "I don't know how to thank you. Will you—will you forgive me?"

"Oh—there's nothing to forgive," said Dick.

"Yes, there is," said Dutton huskily. "I've treated you—I've been a cad, that's what I have! I didn't like you at first—I thought you were proud of your millions. I didn't like the idea of you being here—I was jealous, I guess. I wanted to make you quit. It was I who tied your dog to the saluting gun, and tried to throw the blame on you. I've done other mean things. I—I——"

"Forget it!" said Dick so heartily that the other cadets laughed, and thus broke what was becoming quite a strain.

Major Webster, when he heard the beginning of Dutton's confession, walked away. He was a wise old soldier, and he knew that the lads could best settle those things among themselves.

"And you don't bear me any grudge?" asked Dutton, after a pause.

"Not a bit. But you'd better get back to the hospital and have your ankle looked after," for Dutton was limping.

"Oh, that isn't anything. It might just as well have been my head. But, say, you got a nasty dig."

"Only a scratch," replied Dick with a happy laugh. He would have welcomed another one if it could have insured him such an outcome as had followed this.

"I guess we'd better take you both to the hospital," said Butler, who had ridden up, fearful lest he had seriously injured Dick.

And thither the two wounded cadets were taken, though their stay there was brief.

It was a week after the sensational rescue of Dutton that a meeting of the exclusive society of the Sacred Pig was held in the cosy little club-house which had been built by contributions and donations of the cadets themselves or their fathers. Dutton arose and proposed Dick for membership, the election being unanimous.

The next day being Saturday, was an occasion for the cadets enjoying considerable freedom. It was after the evening parade, when Dick and some of his new chums had received permission to go to town to a theatrical performance, that Major Webster sent for our hero.

"I'll not keep you a moment, Hamilton," he said, "as I know your friends are waiting for you. But you remember that battered marksman's medal that Toots had, and which you requested me to investigate for you?"

"Yes; have you any information about it?"

"I have. I sent it to a friend of mine, an officer at Fort Laramie, Wyoming, and he has just returned it. With it he sends some surprising news."

"What is it?"

"That medal was issued to Corporal William Handlee, a number of years ago."

"Corporal Handlee—the missing soldier—Captain Handlee's son?"

"The very same."

"Why, how—where did Toots get it, I wonder? Is it possible that he——"

"We must ask him. I will question him to-night, and let you know the result. Hark, there he comes now."

Someone was coming down the corridor, whistling the lively strains of "Yankee Doodle."

"That's Toots," said Dick with a smile. "I wonder how he came to have Handlee's medal. Can he possibly be——"

But at that instant there came a series of excited shouts from outside.

"Fire! Fire! Fire!"

Dick and the major rushed to the window.

"Fire! Fire!" shouted Toots, as he ran back along the corridor.

Dick saw a black pall of smoke, through which shot red tongues of flame.

"It's the society house of the Sacred Pig," he cried.

And it was from the windows of the meeting place of the cadets' society that the flames were shooting.

CHAPTER XXXI

DICK WRITES A CHECK—CONCLUSION

As Dick, followed by the major, rushed from the barracks to go to the fire, the housekeeper thrust an envelope into the young millionaire's hand.

"It is a telegram that just came for you," she explained.

Dick shoved it into his pocket without opening it. Then he joined the throng of excited and alarmed students that had gathered about the burning society headquarters.

A small fire department was maintained at the academy, but as the buildings of the school were all fireproof, the brigade was not a very large one, and was only equipped with chemical apparatus.

"We must telephone for the town fire department," cried Dutton.

"They won't get here in time to do much," said Major Webster. "Better save what you can inside, boys."

They saw that what he said was true. There was a stiff wind blowing, fanning the flames to furnace heat. The blaze had started on the upper floor, and had already eaten its way through the roof. No one knew what had caused the fire, as there was no one in the place when it started, and it had burned for some time before breaking out.

Fortunately, the structure was well away from any of the academy buildings, and there was little danger to them.

"Let's save what we can!" cried Dick, and the boys began running in, carrying out such of the trophies as they could find on the lower floor. But it soon became too hot for them, and Major Webster, fearing someone would get hurt, ordered the work of salvage to cease.

"Too bad!" observed Russell Glen, as he and others watched the handsome brick and stone building crumbling into ruins. "And we counted on having such sport there next term."

"Well, it's insured, isn't it?" asked Dick. "We can collect the money, and build a better one."

"Insured!" suddenly cried Dutton. "There, I meant to attend to that, but it slipped my mind!"

"What did?" asked Allen Rutledge.

"The insurance. It expired the day before yesterday."

"And do you mean to say you forgot to get it renewed?"

"I forgot all about it."

"And haven't we a cent of insurance on it?" asked Paul Drew.

"Not a penny. It's all my fault. I meant to get new policies, but I put it off and now——"

"Now it's too late," said Rutledge. "You're a fine treasurer, you are."

Amazement and chagrin made Dutton incapable of replying. The cadets looked on sorrowfully, as they saw their society house being destroyed, knowing that it would be no easy matter to get the money for a new one.

Suddenly there was an explosion from within, and a shower of stones from one of the walls flew into the air.

"Look out!" cried Dick.

He and the others leaped back in time, but Toots, who was in the front rank of spectators, having helped to carry out many valued relics, did not seem to hear. A moment later a fragment of stone struck him on the head, and he fell down.

"Toots is hurt!" cried Dick, running up to the odd janitor, whom all the cadets liked because of his pleasant ways.

"Carry him to the hospital, boys," said the major. "I'll have the surgeon attend to him. Maybe he isn't hurt much."

But from the blood on the head of poor Toots, it would seem that the wound was not a small one.

Sorrowfully Dick and his chums carried the unconscious man. There was little use remaining at the fire now, for it was almost out, having consumed everything save the walls.

"He isn't badly hurt," announced the surgeon cheerfully, when he had examined Toots. "Only a cut on the head. He'll be all right in a few days."

Suddenly the injured man, who had been placed on a couch in the hospital, sat up. He felt of the bandage on his head. Then he looked around wildly.

"Did we beat the red imps off?" he asked. "Why is it I don't hear the firing? Have they retreated? Am I badly hurt? Let me get at 'em again! I'm a good shot! I can pick 'em off!"

He started from his couch, but the surgeon gently pressed him back.

"What's the matter, Toots?" he asked. "Where do you think you are?"

"Toots? Who's Toots? I'm Corporal Bill Handlee, and I must get back to my post. I'm a sharpshooter, and the Indians are attacking us."

The surgeon looked at the injured man in amazement. He thought Toots was delirious. But to Dick the thrilling words meant much. He pressed forward. In his hand he held the battered marksman's medal which Major Webster had returned to him.

"Is this yours, Corporal Handlee?" he asked.

"Yes; where did you get it?" asked Toots. "But why don't some of you speak? Have we beaten off the red imps?"

"Yes," said Dick gently, understanding the whole story now. "They were beaten back some years ago, Toots. Oh, I've found you at last! Won't your father be glad!"

"My father?" and Toots, or, as we must call him now, Corporal Handlee, looked dazed. "My father knows where I am."

"He doesn't, but he soon will," said Dick joyfully, and by degrees, he told the story of how he had agreed to help Captain Handlee locate his missing son, and how, by a strange trick of fate, he had been found.

And that Toots was this missing son there was no doubt. His memory, a blank for many years, because of a bullet wound on the head, received in a fight with the Indians out west, had been restored to him. The surgeon explained it by saying that the blow from the stone, which exploded from the heat, had undone the injury caused by the bullet, by relieving the pressure of a certain bone on the brain. Such cases are rare, but not altogether unknown, he added, and persons who had forgotten for many years who they were suddenly recalled the past.

Of course Toots, or, Corporal Handlee, as we must now call him, could not tell where he had been all the years that he was missing. The last he remembered was taking part in an Indian fight, and being wounded. When he recovered consciousness from the blow of the hot stone, he thought he was still at Fort Lamarie. He had forgotten all the intervening time, including several years spent at Kentfield.

It was surmised that he must have wandered away after the Indian fight, recovered, though with his memory gone, taken another name, and then drifted about, until he secured a place at the military academy. That, the officers recalled, was five years ago.

The corporal had not recognized his own photograph, though something in his hazy memory made him think he knew the man the picture represented. His own medal as a marksman he had supposed belong to another.

"I must send Captain Handlee a telegram at once," said Dick, when the excitement had calmed down. "It will be great news for him."

Leaving Corporal Handlee in charge of the surgeon, the old soldier being quite weak, and hardly able to understand all that had happened, Dick started for the telegraph office, which was not far from the school. He sent the message to the old captain, and, in getting out his money to pay for it, he put his hand in the pocket into which he had thrust the telegram the housekeeper had given him.

"Guess I'd better read it," he murmured. "The fire and finding Corporal Handlee made me forget all about it."

It was from his father, and was very short, but the news it contained made Dick throw his cap up into the air, and yell out in pure delight.

"Wow!" he cried. "Wow! Wow! Wow!"

The operator came running from his little office.

"Got bad news?" he asked.

"Bad?" repeated Dick "No, it's the best in the world! My dad's coming home!"

"Seems to me you're making quite a fuss about it."

"So would you if you knew what else he said," spoke Dick, as he rushed from the building.

He found most of his chums grouped around the ruins of the society house. They were talking about the fire.

"It's all my fault," Dutton was saying. "I guess I'll resign as treasurer."

"I guess we won't have any society, if we can't have a meeting place," observed Hale, sorrowfully.

"Say, Dutton, have you a fountain pen?" asked Dick, as he came up beside his former enemy.

"I guess so. What do you want it for?"

"I'll show you."

Dick sat down on a pile of debris. From his pocket he took a thin, red book, and commenced writing in it by the light of the embers of the ruined society house. Presently he tore out a slip of paper and handed it to Dutton.

"What—what's this?" stammered the treasurer of the Sacred Pig. "Why—why— Hamilton!"

"What is it?" demanded a score of voices, as the cadets crowded up.

"It's a check—a check," stammered Dutton, as he saw the figures which Dick had written in, and noted that they occupied four places. "It's a check!"

"To rebuild the society house of the Sacred Pig," said our hero simply.

"But I—I thought you lost all your money, Hamilton," said Dutton.

"I thought so, too," replied Dick. "So did Uncle Ezra, but I cabled to dad, and it's all a mistake. He took all our funds from the bank that failed before he went abroad. We didn't lose a cent."

"Then you're a millionaire yet, aren't you?" asked Dutton.

"I'm—I'm afraid so," answered Dick.

There was silence for a moment, and then the cadets seemed to understand what Dick had done. They looked at the piece of paper fluttering in Dutton's hand. It meant that they could have a new and better headquarters for their society.

"Three cheers for Dick Hamilton!" called several, and Dick's ears rang to the sweetest music he had ever heard.

They all wanted to shake hands with him at once, and they made so much noise that Colonel Masterly sent one of the teachers out to see if the fire had started afresh.

"It's only the cadets cheering Mr. Hamilton, sir," replied the instructor, when he returned.

"Hum! He's getting to be quite popular," said the colonel, with a smile, for he understood about Dick's handicap.

And there was abundant evidence of his popularity a little later on, for they insisted on carrying Dick on their shoulders to the saluting cannon, where all important events were celebrated, and there they did a sort of war dance about him. Dick would have been glad to escape, but they would not let him.

"We don't want your money, honey, we want you!" they sang. And Dick knew that they spoke the truth. He had fulfilled another condition of his mother's will, and become popular in spite of his wealth, though for a time he feared this would never happen. He had thought of a plan to pretend that he had suddenly grown poor, but Uncle Ezra's mistake made this unnecessary.

"I don't know whether it's more fun to be rich or poor," thought Dick, as he went to bed that night. But he had other adventures, in which his great wealth played a part, and those of you who care to follow Dick Hamilton's fortunes further may read of them in the next volume of this series, to be called: "Dick Hamilton's Steam Yacht; or, A Young Millionaire and the Kidnappers."

"Well, how are you feeling this morning, Toots—I mean Corporal?" asked Dick, about a week later, when the janitor was able to leave the hospital.

"Fine. I'd never know I'd been sick. That was a lucky thing to get hit with a stone, so I could know who I really was. But I'm anxious to get home and see my father, since you say he's not well."

"Oh, he's not seriously ill," said Dick. "I had a letter from Henry Darby about him. He's so pleased that you have been located, that a sight of you is about all the medicine he needs."

"I can go home to him in a few days, Colonel Masterly says."

"You want to give us an exhibition of shooting before you go," suggested Dick.

"I'm afraid I'm all out of practice," objected the former corporal.

But he was not, as he very quickly proved, when he and some chums of Dick went to the rifle range. There the soldier made bullseye after bullseye with an ease that made the cadets fairly gasp, and he did all sorts of fancy shooting, including driving a tack in a board from even a greater distance than even Captain Handlee had boasted that his son could do it.

"I guess it must have been that my eyes were affected by that Indian bullet," said the corporal. "They got all right again when the stone from the fire hit me."

Later, the surgeon admitted that this was probably true.

A short time after this Corporal Bill Handlee joined his aged father in Hamilton Corners, and the two enjoyed many happy years together, thanks to Mr. Hamilton's generosity, and what Dick had done to solve the mystery.

"Well, Grit, old boy," said our hero one day near the close of the term, as he was strolling over the campus, followed by his ugly pet, and with Paul Drew, William the Silent and some other cadets at his side, "well, Grit, I think you and I will go home soon. Dad will be home next week, and say, maybe we won't have some good times; eh, Grit?"

The bulldog nearly turned a summersault to show how glad, he was. A few days later Dick and his dog were at Hamilton Corners, ready for the summer vacation.

End of the book.

www.ingramcontent.com/pod-product-compliance
Lightning Source LLC
Chambersburg PA
CBHW070647290526
45790CB00001B/217